JOURNEYS
INTO
THE
UNKNOWN

Dedicated to Lee Palmisano
"Anything is possible."

How poor the skeptic is, when one realizes that all the people in this world who have had some sort of paranormal experience now believe, and all those who have not yet had such an experience know someone who has.

Table of Contents

Acknowledgments

First and foremost I would like to thank my wife, Michelle, for all her support, hard work, and talent in helping me put this book together. If not for you, where would I be? A special thank you to Catherine Jobe for all her hard work and personal sacrifices on this project. I would also like to thank Tony Hawke and the remarkable staff at the Dundurn Group, my brother Paul Palmisano, who knows just how to capture the reaction he is looking for on tape, and John Perrone, who has amazed me by knowing things we just shouldn't know. Thanks also go to my friends and family who have stood in support of my work.

A special thank you to my good friends and fellow researchers Dee Freedman, Anita Goodrich, Krystal Leigh, and Alison Hann for their participation and hard work on some of the projects within this book, and for their opinions and insight into things that go bump in the night.

Thank you to my good friends Dave and Susan Billingham for their encouragement and generous support; to John Mullan for all his sharing of technical insight, direction, and the ability to build anything; to Michael Nguyen for his work and technical support; to Darrin Lapointe for his valued opinions; and to Peter McSherry, who seems to know the history of everything.

To the junior team, Laura, Suzi, and Sara Hann and Jessica and Jaymi Goodrich: education and an open mind will hold the answers.

Anyone wishing to contact me regarding questions, comments, or personal tales of their own encounters may do so at overshadows@sympatico.ca. Please do not send emails with attachments, as these will unfortunately be deleted before they reach me.

Introduction

You walk up the pathway, laden with heavy packs of equipment; it's just turning dark, and the rain is cold on your face. You stop at the front door, putting the packs down and searching for the key. Your mind is racing, trying to remember the layout beyond the door and, more importantly, the location of the nearest light switch. The door arches open, and you stumble in. You freeze, as something is moving on the hardwood floor a few feet from where you stand. You can see the light switch in the fading beams of weak sun that filter in through the open door behind you. Beyond the switch, nothing but blackness and that noise. Now comes the major decision: go for the switch or back out the door and leave. The stories revolving around this house spiral through your brain, and you know that according to your preliminary investigation something lurks in there, in the dark beyond that switch, waiting and watching with unknown intentions. You step forward and reach out, flicking on the switch. Dull yellow light invades the shadow, pushing it off into the corners of the hall and surrounding room, making the deeper interior of the house look even more shrouded in pitch darkness. You pick up the packs and place them in the hall, taking out a flashlight and firing a beam deep into the main floor of the house. You proceed inside with caution, looking for light switches, knowing that you are the trespasser, for whatever lingers here lived and died in this house long before you came onto the scene. You hope your research partner will show up soon, but you proceed, because that's the commitment you made when you decided to call yourself a paranormal investigator.

Ghosts, apparitions, and spirits — what are they and why are they here? Are they simply a glimpse into the past? Are they the souls of the dearly departed, continuing with their lives on the other side? Do they have a more profound meaning, or are they simply bits of information floating around the ether? Maybe they don't even exist. Could it all be hallucinations brought on by standing waves, solar flares, or forms of dementia? If so, then medical science has certainly missed a huge drug market, as those brave enough to come forward to tell their stories range in the multiples of millions over the last one hundred years and include military personnel, elected officials, captains of industry, and, yes, even scientists. Skeptics like to toss around the word *hallucination* when it comes to people reporting ghostly phenomena. They feel this concept, which most people know very little about, is an acceptable explanation. The fact of the matter is that science knows very little about what causes a hallucination. However, doctors and scientists all agree on a common list of causes: high and prolonged fever; intoxication from illicit drugs or alcohol; delirium or dementia; brain damage or brain cancer; severe medical conditions such as liver or kidney failure; psychotic disorders such as schizophrenia, psychotic depression, and post-traumatic stress disorder; and sensory deprivations like blindness and/or deafness. According to health care workers in Canada, hallucinations are rare in healthy, active people. I've tried to acquire some statistics on multiple and mass hallucinations; oddly, there are none, yet I've heard the term used to describe multiple witnesses to paranormal events many times. Skeptics are quick to tell you there is little basis in science to claim ghosts exist, yet they feel it is easy to explain them away using terms and ideas that are nothing more than pseudo-science themselves. It is very curious that if these experiences were hallucinations, they seemed to affect many witnesses to a single event. It also seems that these hallucinations can affect audio and video equipment, as well as a large array of other scientific devices, which, in some cases, verify what the witness has reported. Some of the greatest scientists of our time have theorized the existence of life after death — Einstein, Edison, Tesla, and Marconi to name a few. It is extremely unnerving to think that these people, who gave us so much, suffered from dementia, according to the logic of the skeptic. I have, over my travels, had the opportunity to talk with several well-entrenched skeptics about the study of the paranormal (specifically life after death) and what, in their eyes, would constitute proof. They all agree that if we could bring the spirit into the lab and have it repeat its actions and abilities under scientific conditions they would believe, and that is where I am at a loss, for the spirits of the dead are quite uncooperative. I can't imagine anyone convincing one to enter a laboratory to perform like a stage dog anytime soon. So we plod along. The proof exists out there in field investigations and observations. The bottom line is time. Time to investigate means being persistent and staying on one case as long as possible, with constant surveillance and attempts at interaction. With this, the dead will give up their secrets. Our actions at the location of a haunting will energize their interest and excite their emotions, which in time will allow them to manifest and attempt to communicate with us, bringing us ever closer to the answers we seek.

A Few Thoughts

I am in no sense of the word a "ghostbuster." I hate the term. The people I work with and I consider ourselves mediators. We attempt to investigate the problems of both parties, the living and the dead, and try to apply conflict resolution techniques to the situation. The complaints of the living normally include fear of perceived activity that may be taking place in their dwelling, however this activity may manifest itself. The complaints of the dead are, by their very nature, not so easily definable. They may range from something that the people are doing within the dwelling, to renovations of the structure, to the placement of some article that the spirit may object to. It is our task, once asked for help, to seek out the root of these problems and find a solution by which both parties can exist in relatively peaceful harmony.

To "ghostbust" is to attack, confront, and make an outright attempt to force a spirit out of a dwelling. This may seem like a desirable outcome, but let's consider several things. First, the spirit was more than likely there first and has a strong connection with the place. It may not have anywhere else to go. Second, we have no significant proof to show why spirits are here in the first place; it may be for a specific reason. Third, we have seen, in some cases, a balance of benevolent and malevolent spirits dwelling in the same place, providing a balance of power over each other. To remove one is to destroy that balance; remove the wrong one and you may face the full onslaught of the malevolent ones.

The attempt to categorize ghosts and spirits by their actions adds to the confusion when trying to investigate activity. As rationally thinking humans, living within our organized society, we like to compartmentalize everything in our lives. This thinking works for some things, but not for ghosts. We have to remember that they, like us, are individuals and as such have intelligence, emotions, and self-motivation. All of this makes each one of them different from the next, regardless of what we perceive as a witness or investigator. Until we realize this we will not be able to make a meaningful connection and come to an understanding of why they do what they do. We will be trapped between curiosity and fear, and they will become frustrated.

A Special Note

When psychics make contact with spirit energy there is an unexplainable change within their brainwave patterns. Where they are awake, conscious, walking around, and talking, their normal brainwave patterns should be within the beta frequency range, 14 to 30 hertz (Hz). However, when they establish contact, their brainwave patterns fall into the low theta frequency range, 4 to 7 Hz, and on rare occasions into the high delta frequency range, 0.5 to 3.5 Hz. It is interesting to note that theta is the dominant brainwave pattern in children under four years old.

I believe this change in brainwave frequency allows psychics to perceive and communicate with energies that exist on the fringes of our normal reality. The psychic normally receives information and images in their mind from the spirit or spirits present. From time to time, within some of our investigations, there are sessions of communication using a pendulum. The psychic uses the pendulum as a tool to focus and enhance the information being received into direct questions and answers.

The Stories

The following is a collection of stories from people who attest to the validity of the events. They have been compiled from several sources, including several stories that occurred under the watchful eye of security professionals who, while executing their duties to protect people and property, have been drawn into unexplainable events.

The Little Girl and the Thing in the Basement
Scarborough

It started not long after they moved into a detached two-bedroom bungalow on a quiet residential street between Lawrence and Ellesmere.

The house was built in the late 1960s as part of a subdivision. There was nothing in its relatively short history to indicate there would be any problems of this nature. The young couple, Ed and June, had been living together for several years and were considering marriage. She worked for a bank, and he was employed by a local police force.

One summer evening, as the couple sat in the living room watching a movie, there came a knock from the basement, from just below where they sat. They just looked at each other. Two more knocks followed. Ed moved off the couch to the carpeted floor above the sound and knocked back twice. Two knocks came in return. He paused, looking at her in astonishment. He knocked again in a pattern: *tap, tap, tap,* pause, *tap, tap.* After a moment came the response: *tap, tap, tap ... tap, tap.*

June stood by the phone, prepared to call for help as he went down the basement stairs, looking for the prankster. Nothing out of the ordinary was found, and all the windows were locked. The knocks from the basement continued on a regular basis. Not long after they started to notice, to their fright, that something would come up to the main floor from the basement. At 11:15 every night there would be walking on the stairs from the basement to the kitchen, then something would move around the kitchen for a couple of minutes, the floor creaking underfoot. Then it would leave, heading back down to the basement. The disturbance never lasted longer than three minutes, but it was the longest, scariest three minutes ever, as they never knew if it would change its pattern and come into the living room or bedroom with them. The first time they tested this she went into the kitchen; a knot grew in the pit of her stomach, but she didn't see anything. Then a metal serving tray jumped off a shelf on the wall, flew past her, rattled off the opposite wall, and landed on the floor. The tins that stood in front of the tray on the shelf were undisturbed. She immediately left the house.

When they informed company about the nightly visitor they were met with skepticism, until 11:15 p.m. Strangely, neither the skeptics nor the believers ever arose and went into the kitchen to see what was making the noise. "You just had this feeling in your gut warning you not to go in there!" they said.

Ed was about to switch to night shift, and unfortunately this meant that there were going to be times when June would be home alone. This prospect wasn't very appealing to her in view of these strange incidences. They agreed to install a security alarm system throughout the house. Ed picked up all the components and wiring and, along with his brother-in-law, wired all the windows and doors and added motion detectors. He also added security bars inside all of the basement windows. June felt at least a little safer staying alone in the house. Should things continue to happen, her parents didn't live far away, and her father could be at the house in under twenty minutes.

They bought a three-month-old cocker spaniel who had made a very impressive argument with them at the pet shop, wrapping herself around their legs and just hamming it up. From Bug's introduction to the house she seemed to interact with something that they couldn't see. Ed and June would, from time to time, buy the dog a rawhide shaped like a shoe, which Bug enjoyed. One day they arrived home after work to find that every shoe had been removed from the hall closet and laid heel to toe, snaking through the living room and dining room, with the rawhide shoe right at the lead. Now, either something very odd was going on or this dog was destined for Hollywood. On another occasion they had ordered Chinese food. The dog just loved those dry noodles that were meant to be added to the chow mein. As a treat, she would get a couple of these. This particular night the noodles were forgotten and left aside with the condiments. In the morning, the bag of noodles was missing, but nothing was thought of it until a few days later. While Ed was playing with Bug, pulling toys out of her toy box, he found the empty noodle bag buried deep under the toys, hidden. The bag hadn't been chewed, but rather opened quite carefully. The staple still hung from its unfolded corner.

They set up a small office in the basement, and June spent time down there working on the computer. There was a large chair in the corner of the room behind her. The dog would sit and look up at the empty chair, sometimes resting her head on the seat as if she were being petted. She would also bring her ball and toys to the chair.

During the day the house seemed comfortable, but when the sun went down, especially when the hour neared 11:00 p.m., the uneasy feelings came over them. They never dared to go down to the basement after dark. One day they were having a yard sale and a barbecue for friends, and June decided to do a couple loads of laundry at the same time. Later that night, after everyone had left and they were tidying up, she mentioned she had forgotten a load in the washer. Ed looked at the clock — 10:50 p.m. — walked to the top of the basement stairs, and stood there a moment. He went to the fridge and took out a barbecued pork chop. He waved it under Bug's nose and the animal went wild, doing every trick she knew. He knew she would practically kill for such a treat, so he said, "You want it, go get it!" and tossed it down the base-ment stairs. The dog rushed to the stairs and slid to a stop at the top; looking down those stairs at the pork chop, she let out a whimper, turned, and walked away, heading into the living room. That was good enough for him; he looked into the bedroom and told her that the laundry would have to wait until the morning.

The knocks from the basement continued; after Ed had left the house for work they became violent, no longer just a series of knocks but pounding that sounded like everything in the basement was being destroyed. June would call her parents' house and wait outside on the street for her father to arrive. He would check the place. Nothing was ever found to be dis-turbed. Nothing seemed to help; even the security built into the house didn't stop the noises emanating from the basement. The only thing it proved was that it wasn't a neighbourhood prankster.

One afternoon when Ed and June arrived home from grocery shopping, he opened the side door and they were stopped dead in their tracks by a blood-curdling scream from the basement. They both backed away from the door and stood in the driveway, looking at each other. After a few moments, he slipped into the house and began his search. Again, nothing was found. This episode was extremely unnerving to both of them. It was at this time they started to seriously discuss moving away, but it just wasn't financially sensible at the time to move.

One night they were sleeping soundly when something started talking to June, rousing her from her sleep. Just as she opened her eyes, the talking stopped. She immediately woke Ed up. He jumped from the bed and grabbed for the baseball bat, flicking on the light. He was thinking of a living, breathing intruder and went on a search, until he realized that the alarm system hadn't gone off. He checked the panel and there was nothing but green lights. He came back into the bedroom and found June standing in the doorway, terrified. Nothing was found, and she couldn't tell what had been said. Neither of them slept that night.

A few weeks later Ed's mother arrived for a visit and was going to spend the weekend at the house. That night, after they had all gone to bed, the banging started in the basement. Two things were different that night: only Ed's mother and the dog heard it, and it was extremely volatile. Bug dove onto the bed with Ed's mother and trembled with fear, and the banging actually shook the bed. Someone appeared at her bedroom door and said something; she couldn't hear it clearly over the banging. The person was cloaked in shadow. In the morning, she questioned them about what had happened the night before. They didn't offer an explanation, and she kept insisting that it had been June at the bedroom door.

About a week later, around 5:30 a.m., as Ed sat in the car in the driveway warming it up, he glanced at the side door to the house and, to his astonishment, saw what appeared to be a young girl bounding up the stairs to the main floor, her long pigtails swinging back and forth. He turned off the car and entered the house. He found no sign of the girl, and his wife still slept soundly, but the dog sat by the couch quietly. He knew what he had seen, yet he could find nothing that would prove it. He looked back at the dog, who was now resting her head against the couch. He briefly considered waking his wife, but then quickly dismissed it as a bad idea — "Honey, something's running around the house, got to go to work, bye!" — so he let her sleep and went off to work.

One night, Ed's brother and his girlfriend came over for dinner, and as the evening wore on they started to discuss the events in the house. The girlfriend suggested that they all go downstairs to confront it; she was making fun of them and was skeptical of the whole idea. It was around 10:30 p.m. when they went downstairs, against the couple's better judgment. June pulled up a barstool and sat down, facing the bottom of the stairs. There came a heavy bang from upstairs. Bug took off to investigate, leaving them downstairs. She said, "Wouldn't it be funny if the dog's ball came down the stairs?" Before she could finish the sentence, the ball bounced down the stairs. A few moments later the dog started down the stairs, tight up against the wall as if squeezing past something blocking her path. Halfway down, the dog stopped and urinated on the landing. This was completely uncharacteristic, as she would never go to the bathroom in the house. The girlfriend yelled, "If you are there show yourself!" There was a noise on the landing. June was unable to blink, her eyes glazed over, and she started to fall off the stool backwards. They caught her and held her up. They followed her gaze to the landing, and there stood a figure blacker than the shadows, piercing blue eyes fixed on her. They all started screaming, "Enough!" and "Go away!" while quickly turning on the lights. She snapped out of whatever had been happening to her. The figure was gone. They ran up the stairs, slamming the basement door closed and retreating to the living room. There they sat for a while, no one speaking until Ed's brother and his girlfriend left.

The events terrified them, and no matter how hard they tried they just couldn't find a solution. Whatever dwelled in the basement had won. They decided it could have the place, and they packed and moved far away from that house.

The Playful and the Disturbed
Toronto

The house was originally built in the late 1890s as a farmhouse. In 1956, the area became part of a housing development. The farmhouse was moved back two hundred feet to a new foundation, where it currently sits, so that the subdivision road could be straightened. The house was incorporated into the new development, and brickwork was added around the original wood structure. There are windows on the outside of the house that do not exist inside. The owner mentioned that when a small bathroom renovation was done and a wall was replaced, they found an eighteen-inch air space between the original interior wall and the outside brick wall. She said you could see from the upper floor down into the foundation of the house when looking down into the space.

While speaking to the owner of the house, I learned that she, her husband, and their five sons have lived there since 1965. Her husband and one son are now deceased. The first thing they wanted to show me was the rose bush. One of the sons, who takes care of the property and gardens, observed something that he brought to the rest of the family. In the mid-1980s the father planted a rose bush along the fence line. The bush grew but never bloomed. It seemed like a lost cause, but no one ever bothered pulling out the bush. In the early 1990s the father passed away, and since his death that bush has yielded wonderful flowers. They continue to bloom to this very day. As we went to the basement, she told me about the time she went downstairs to put a load of laundry on. As she neared the back door to the laundry room, she heard what seemed to be a loud party, people talking and laughing. She could also hear the sound of glass on glass. She paused for a long time, just listening to the sounds. Then, when she felt brave enough, she pulled open the door and found nothing but her empty laundry room. All the sounds had stopped abruptly.

She pointed out the washroom where not only the residents but also countless visitors have had similar experiences. While using that washroom, they have heard phantom knocks at the door and loud fits of coughing in the basement. Everyone reported the same thing; as soon as they went into the washroom the knocking would start, only to be interrupted by coughing. This normally caused the person in the washroom to rush, but when they came out they would find that no one else was there and no one had come down the basement stairs behind them. Most relatives who visit now will use only the washroom on the upper floor.

I was introduced to the middle son, who is now in his late forties. He remembers an incident that occurred when he was living there. He was coming from the bathroom and had just started to go up the stairs when a hand from behind grabbed him firmly on the shoulder. He states that he will never forget the way that squeeze felt. He turned around and found nothing there.

I asked the woman if the basement seemed to be the focal point of all the phenomena occurring in the house. She just looked at me for a moment. "No, it's all throughout the house. There have been so many things that have happened over the years that it's hard to remember them all. I remember having tea with my youngest son one evening at the kitchen table when we heard a frightful yell for help, it was very clear. It was a child crying for help and it came up from the basement. It scared both of us, so I called my oldest son to come with us to look in the basement. We searched, but nothing was found."

As we made our way up to the main floor she told me about the visitor who, from time to time, comes up from the basement to the main floor. "It could be heard in the middle of the night: *thump, thump, thump*, up the stairs. It would stop here for a few moments." She showed me how the floor squeaks near the top of the stairs, by the stove in the kitchen. "Then it walks up and down the hall from the kitchen to the front door and back. This goes on for a few minutes, and then it goes back downstairs." I asked her how often this happens. She said, "From time to time. … It really gets active as we get closer to Christmas." Why Christmas? She just shrugged her shoulders.

"We also have someone who comes in the back door on very rare occasions; they walk down the hall and go straight upstairs. One night my father was over visiting; he, my husband, my youngest son, and I were all in the living room watching a show and talking when someone came in the back door. They walked down the hall and past the living room and went running up the stairs. My husband asked 'Who was that?' I thought it was my eldest son, so I went out to the bottom of the stairs, and the family dog followed me. I looked up, but there were no lights on up there, it was pitch black. The dog started up the first two stairs, then whimpered and jumped back down to the landing and looked up the stairs. He cried and I noticed his tail was down, between his legs. My husband came out to see why the dog was crying. He just looked at me and I guess he sensed something wasn't right. He flicked on the light switch and called up the stairway, 'Who's up there?' Then he went up to have a look. By this time everyone was in the hall, except the dog, which had gone back to the living room and was watching us from the doorway. My father followed my husband up and in a few minutes came back down. They hadn't found anything."

We went up the stairs to the upper floor. I had a look around; there were three bedrooms and a bathroom. She pointed out the smallest bedroom. "This is the one with most of the problems. My sons used it when they lived at home, then it became a guest room. Now I just use it for storage. My sons used to tell me about voices coming from the closet and out from under the bed. A guest also told me about a voice from the closet. She thought it was someone in the hall, but when she looked there was no one there. My oldest son had an incident in that room. He had just gone to bed and had rolled over to face the wall when bright light came from behind him, filling the room. He became paralyzed and very cold. He tried to shake and wiggle out of whatever it was, and he tried to call for help, but couldn't. All the while, I was just in the next room. After a while, he wasn't sure how long, he was finally able to cry out, and my husband and I went to see what the trouble was. We had to turn him over; he was cold and still couldn't move so I called an ambulance and we took him to the hospital. They ran all kinds of tests on him and kept him overnight. The doctor couldn't offer any explanations, since the tests showed nothing was wrong." This happened to two of her other sons over the next few years, each time in that same room. They all said the same thing; they believed there was someone in the room with them, even though they could not see anyone. "My husband was a very rational man, he served in the Canadian Army in the Second World War. He never talked about this stuff and I don't know if he believed any of it, but after all these problems with that room, he decided to sleep in there. I remember the next morning. I came down to the kitchen early; he was already up, sitting at the table having his second cup of coffee. I just looked at him, and he took me into his confidence, knowing I wouldn't say anything to the kids. He said it was fairly late when he heard the voice under the bed, talking … but nothing was there. After he searched he tried to ignore it, but it was annoying. Then he heard the closet door creak and something jumped out at him. It looked like a black shadow. He threw his legs up in defence and nothing came, no impact, nothing. He felt shaken and foolish at the same time. He just laid there for a while, then came down to the kitchen. In all the years I had known him I had never seen him that way." I asked her what they did after that. She looked at me and said, "We just stood our ground. This was our home and we raised our family here; there was no way we were going to leave! I'll tell you this: he tore that entire closet out. It's now the only bedroom without a closet."

A Playful Spirit Enjoys Playing Mischievous Games

The owner of the house prepared her bath. It had been a long, hard day and she just wanted to relax. She placed her towel on the hook and was about to step into the tub when there came a knock at the bathroom door. She grabbed her towel and opened the door, knowing the only other person in the house was her husband. No one was there, so she dismissed it as imagination. Again, she was about to step into the tub when the lights went out in the room. She fumbled around and opened the door, noticing that the switch, which was located in the hall, was turned off. She checked the upstairs floor more thoroughly and found nothing. She shook her head and went back to her bath. She stepped in and felt the warm water around her feet when there was another knock at the door. No one was there. She made her way downstairs and into the living room, where her husband had dozed off in front of the television. She woke him and gave him a piece of her mind, blaming him for the games and interruptions to her bath. He just looked at her and in his passive way said nothing in return, watching her storm back up the stairs to return to the bathroom. There were no further interruptions.

Christmas Spirits

It was late in the evening on December 24. The family was together for the holidays. One son had arrived with his wife and children from out west. The occupants of the house were used to the odd sounds and unseen things moving around late at night. They had all said their good-nights and retired to their rooms. It wasn't long before the noises started downstairs. Someone clomped up the basement stairs to the kitchen. The sound of walking could be heard moving up and down the main floor hall, again stopping in the kitchen, followed by the sound of a spoon stirring in a cup. One of the young girls, age six, in the guest room was still awake with excitement and said aloud, "Mommy, listen, it's Santa." The mother said, "That's right dear, now go to sleep." Everyone stayed in bed and listened. The noises stopped as the footfalls receded back down the basement stairs.

On Christmas Day, after driving his grandmother home, the youngest son walked through the back door into the kitchen. He paused; everyone sat, very quietly, looking at him. He felt something was very wrong. Then, from upstairs, came the bangs, as if someone were going through dresser drawers and slamming them closed. He quickly scanned the room, but no one seemed to be missing. "Who's upstairs?" he asked.

His brother looked at him and said, almost in a whisper, as if he didn't want whoever was up there to hear, "We don't know."

"How long has it been going on?" he asked.

"A few minutes," his mother said.

"Well, we should have a look," he said to the room as he headed down the hall. His brother reluctantly followed. They stopped at the foot of the stairs and peered up to the second floor. Pitch-blackness was all there was; not a single light was on up there. He flicked on the upper hall light, and the banging paused. They headed up the stairs. All the rooms were black, and fear held them in place for a moment. They went from room to room, turning on every light, searching everywhere. At the end of it all nothing out of the ordinary was found.

It wasn't long after Christmas that the adults wanted to go out together. The youngest son volunteered to stay back and babysit his niece. The group left around 6:30 p.m. and planned to return before 11:00 p.m. The evening began uneventfully; he talked with a friend on the phone while the child watched a movie in the living room.

He hung up the phone and gave the girl a drink, then ran upstairs to retrieve his cigarettes from his room. It was just starting to get dark, but he had enough light to see his way up the stairs to his room without turning on the hall light. As usual, in this house, you tried to observe everything and keep your eyes open. He noticed as he got to the top of the stairs that all the bedroom doors were wide open, which was normal. He went into his room and picked up the smokes and lighter, pausing to look at something on his dresser. Within a split second there came a noise, then a scream from the stairs. He turned and stepped out of his room just in time to see his niece, who was halfway up the stairs, turn and catapult off the seventh stair. She flew through the air, landing hard on the floor and slamming into the front door of the house. He rushed down the stairs to see if she was injured. As he did he noticed the bathroom light was on and the door was ajar by maybe three inches. He picked her up; she was hysterical but uninjured. He tried to help her calm down. Finally, between breaths, she said that someone was upstairs in the bathroom and that as she went up, she heard them make a noise. When she turned to see what the noise was they were crouched down, peeking through the opening at her. He realized that she had never made it to the top of the stairs, yet the light was off and the door was open when he first went up. Fear washed over him, as he now felt an intruder was in the house.

He looked up, and the bathroom light was now off. He took the child to the back door and opened it, then picked up the phone and called a friend who lived a few doors away, asking him to come over immediately. When the friend arrived he quickly explained what was happening and told him that he was going to check the upper floor. He wanted him to go directly to the neighbours with the girl to call the police. Before anyone could move, a loud pounding started upstairs. It sounded like someone was bouncing the end of a baseball bat off the hardwood floor. They stood there, listening with fear. They were about to leave when a car pulled up and the family emerged. He told them what had happened, and the men entered the house. All was quiet. They cautiously climbed the stairs, turning on the lights as they went. The place was searched from top to bottom. Nothing was found.

He was twelve at the time. It was a Saturday and he had woken early, but had stayed in bed enjoying the warm blankets and cool air of the room. The family had a wirehair dachshund who was sleeping on the bed at his master's feet. The boy shifted and the dog lifted his head; they looked at each other. In that moment, when their eyes met, the dog spoke. The boy's response was to kick the dog in fear, sending it tumbling from the bed. He stated that the voice had been harsh and low, but very clear. I asked what it had said. He looked at me and told me it had said only one word: "Venue!"

I asked him what he thought that meant, and he just shrugged his shoulders. I went to the Oxford Dictionary and found two definitions: "1. The place where something happens. 2. District where a criminal or civil case must be heard." What it meant here was unclear. He added that the voice sounded like an old man. I asked him what happened to the dog. He said, "After he hit the floor, he just got up and walked out of the room." The dog was fine.

Exactly a month after the dog incident the boy again woke up early. He went downstairs to get a drink. Afterwards, he decided that he would go back to bed for a little while, at least until someone else was awake. He climbed back into bed and lay there for a few minutes. He rolled over onto his stomach, and as he did so the bedcovers were ripped off of him and he felt two hands grab his feet. He screamed and twisted to see who it was. No one was there, but he could still feel the hands, and their grip tightened. They started to pull him from the bed and he fought back, kicking and clawing at the mattress, trying to hang on. He was losing the battle and started to be pulled off the end. His T-shirt slid in the opposite direction and soon covered his face; he admitted this was the absolute height of his panic, and in that panic he fought for his life.

Someone was up and moving in the hall just outside his room, and as he heard them, whatever it was vanished. He jumped up, pulled his T-shirt down, and scanned the room. The blankets lay in a heap on the floor, but nothing was in the room. He rushed out of the room and went downstairs to be with whoever was up. It was his mother. He sat at the dining room table and said nothing about the incident. As she made tea, he studied the red handprints around his ankles.

It was almost 11:00 p.m. when there was a knock at the door. The mother answered and let her youngest son's friends in. She called her son down from his bedroom and asked, "Why are your friends here so late on a work night?" They explained that there was a very bad situation at their house; they had to leave and had nowhere to go. They wanted to know if they could borrow his sleeping bag as they were going to stay in the local park. He felt bad for them and spoke to his mother, and she immediately offered them a place to stay, since it was around 15° Celsius outside. He went to get his sleeping bag and a blanket for them and led them to the living room. He told them to be quiet, as his parents had to get up early for work. They said good night, and he returned to his room.

Around 2:00 a.m. he awoke to a blaring TV and the sound of running in the hall. He went downstairs in a rush to find his friends putting on their shoes at the back door. He turned the TV off and asked them what was going on. They told him that they were just lying there talking about their situation when the TV guide flipped up into the air and off the coffee table, followed by the TV going on full blast by itself. There was no one else in the room, but they felt as though there were. They thanked him for having them but said they were going to stay in the park. With that, they left the warmth and safety of the house and, with his sleeping bag in hand, went off to brave the cold rather than stay in the house.

He checked the room again, finding nothing out of the ordinary.

Waking the Dead
Burlington

Jeff worked security on the night shift for four years. When the sun went down the warehouse and small electronics repair shop became his responsibility. He knew everything about the eighteen-thousand-square-foot complex. It was just after a major renovation that unusual things began to occur. He admits that it doesn't really bother him, as he finds little bits of mystery and excitement help pass the late night hours. He recalls nothing in the building's history that would account for the strange things that go on. The building is relatively new, no one died there, and everything was quiet until three months earlier. He believes that the unusual events all started during the renovations, when they moved walls and cut the floor to relocate the bathrooms.

The first time something strange was noticed was on a weekend. Jeff came in to relieve the day shift security officer; he was walking from the front door to the rear of the building, down a long corridor, and the other officer was walking up to greet him. When they were within a few feet of the bathrooms they both heard the sinks turn on and the urinals flush in the men's washroom. Jeff looked at his colleague and asked, "Who's in there?"

The other security officer just shot him an odd look and said, "No one, we are the only two in the building." He handed Jeff the emergency phone and headed for the front door.

"Are you going to check?" Jeff asked.

"Don't want to know!" he said, and with that he left. Jeff stopped outside the washroom door and listened; all was quiet. He pushed the door open and stepped in, slowly moving to the toilet stalls. Nothing. The three sinks and four urinals were all connected to individual motion detectors. He tested them, and they all seemed to work properly.

I was introduced to Mary, who works the reception desk. She says she hates the bathroom. On several occasions she has been in there and heard whispering in the next stall. At first, she thought someone was in there on a cellphone, but after closer inspection she discovered that she was alone.

She confided that she has felt oppressed in there. "If the restaurant wasn't so far away, I'd drive there to use their washroom instead," she said.

Jeff agrees that the bathrooms are the focal point for whatever is going on, but the activity is not confined to that area. Workers have reported doors closing on them just as they are about to pass through the open doorway. Products keep falling off a small section of storage rack. The warehouse supervisor can't explain why things fall off this section of rack; it has cost the company a great deal of money in damaged stock. Extra care was taken when placing products up there after the problem was noticed, yet it kept occurring. An outside engineering firm has inspected the rack and tested it for vibrations. The rack is bolted into the concrete floor and is perfectly level. The product in question is normally a TV monitor in a crate, which weighs between thirty-five and forty pounds, and the crates are placed onto wood pallets, where there is no overhang at all. They could not find any reasonable explanation.

Eric was the first to see the black shadow. "It was as big as a man and moved in the hall between the washrooms. It wasn't something I wanted to see, it scared me, and I don't like going into that washroom."

Jeff said, "One of the scariest times for me was the night the cleaners encountered it." He added, "The cleaners, a married Spanish couple, came in like any other night. I opened the offices for them. After a few minutes she went to work on the bathrooms and I led the man to the repair shop to unlock the door for him. Just as we were arriving at the shop, his wife, screaming in Spanish, came running into the warehouse. I didn't know what to expect, so we ran back to where she was.

"She stated that she was cleaning the sinks in the men's bathroom when the motion sensor on the furthest sink turned on, and as she looked up, a black shadow of a person was reflected in the mirror beside her. They were looking at me, like I was trained to deal with something like this! It took us a few minutes to gather the courage to go in and have a look around. I led, followed by the man, then his wife. It was funny, they had all this faith in me, and I was thinking to myself, sure hope nothing is in here because these cleaners are going to be in the way of my exit. Luckily, nothing was found."

Other staff members have reported strange shadows that move around between the office and the washrooms, sometimes venturing out into the warehouse. More than half of the time they see it in the reflection of some surface like a monitor or mirror, only to turn and find nothing. It is always fleeting; most don't even report it, as they aren't sure of what they saw.

Jeff looked serious as he told me the story. "I did finally see this thing; it was one night after the cleaners had left the building and they had propped the washroom doors open to let the floor dry. I was coming from the warehouse to the office to make some coffee. When the door is open to the woman's washroom you can see a portion of a large mirror, as well as a one-and-a-half-inch bevel on its edge. As I was walking past the door, I happened to look in and this black thing was reflected in the bevel. It seemed to be moving, almost shimmering. That made me feel very uncomfortable and I spent most of the night outside. Now I insist that the cleaners keep those doors closed when they are done."

I asked if he knew what was on the site prior to the warehouse being built. "Nothing but field for as long as I can remember," he said. Jeff thinks that when the contractors cut the floor, they may have disturbed a grave lost to time.

George had a habit of coming into work early to get a head start on the day's workload. One morning he had just settled in and was answering some e-mails when he heard whispering coming from just outside his office door. He went out to see who it was, but could find no one. He returned to his desk, and as he sat down he saw something like a black shadow, the size of an average person, walk very deliberately past his office door. He got up from his desk and went out into the outer office to see who it was, thinking that he had to have initially missed whoever was in; again no one was there. He checked with security to find out who else was in the building, but other than George and the security officer no one else was in yet.

It was about a week later that George was in his office in the early morning working. He heard some noises in the outer office, so he got up and went to investigate. His search revealed only that he was alone.

He returned to his desk, and as he started to go over some schedules he heard a man's voice directly behind him whisper into his ear, "Do I scare you?" George jumped up and rushed to the security office to report the incident; again security and George were the only people in the building. George now refuses to come in early.

It was late in the evening; Frank and Tom were working late, trying to catch up on some work. The only other person in the warehouse was the security officer. As Frank counted stock he saw who he thought was Tom walking two aisles over. He called to him, but there was no response, he just kept walking. Frank put the box he was working on back on the shelf and headed up the aisle to meet up with Tom, but at the end of the row he found himself alone. He knew it wasn't security he had seen because of the uniform colours. He stormed into Tom's office to ask him why he hadn't acknowledged his calls. Tom just looked at him and told him that he hadn't left his office in almost an hour.

Was He a Ghost?
Toronto

Jim was a security supervisor at a large apartment complex at Yonge and Eglinton. He heard I was doing a book on the paranormal and called me. I met him at his office and he introduced me to several of his staff, who told me about an incident that had occurred in the building. It was late December, and there had been a rash of break and enters in the area. The tenants' association had requested that extra security staff be brought in and patrols increased. It was just after 4:00 in the afternoon when a tenant called down to the front desk, reporting something strange on the tenth floor. He said it was an intruder and security should come immediately. The supervisor and four officers responded. As they arrived, someone at the end of the hall ran from an apartment door towards the stairwell. Three officers jumped back on the elevator and went down, two of them getting off at the sixth floor, the other going to the ground floor to watch the stairwell fire exit. The two officers on the sixth floor split up, each taking a stairwell, one north, one south, both heading up. Meanwhile, the supervisor and other officer made for the north stairwell, where they had seen this person run. As they entered the stairwell they could hear someone running up, and they gave chase. They called on the radio to the other officers, advising them of their location and direction. Up they went, all officers converging towards whoever this was. They were passing the last tenant floor and could still hear him running upward. They knew they had him, as the only remaining floors now were mechanical and the roof, both of which were locked. He had nowhere to go.

Security stopped dead as a terrifying noise came down towards them, followed by a twisted four-inch heavy-duty steel fire door hinge, which crashed into the stair landing near one officer. They proceeded up slowly, fading sunlight now evident at the roof level. They arrived to find the steel fire door twisted and ripped from the wall like a flimsy piece of tin, cast aside. The doorway leading to the roof gaped open, but the snow beyond the door was perfect and undisturbed. They were about to go onto the roof when the officer in the lobby called up and advised them that two police officers were on site. He brought them up, and the seven of them went out to the roof and searched, but nothing was found.

The tenant was questioned about what he had seen. He knew the person who lived in the apartment where the incident had started, and knew that he was away for Christmas. He said had seen a black shadow, which seemed to have passed through the apartment door several times, then back out into the hall. It had no features and looked very strange. He felt frightened by it, and when he called down didn't know what to say, so he just said the first thing that popped into his head: "Intruder!"

The supervisor handed me a copy of the original report, a copy of the police report, and a file folder with reports from 1981, detailing that a man had committed suicide in that very apartment. Was it related? The supervisor believed so.

He told me about the many reports about strange occurrences in that unit, people moving in then moving out quickly, breaking their leases. Some had even fled in the middle of the night, sending movers to pack up their belongings.

He then introduced me to a woman in her late seventies who had lived in that unit for three weeks. She now lives three floors lower in the building. When asked about the apartment she became very stone-faced, looking at me for a long moment. "That place should be sealed, no one should be allowed in there. I moved in and right from the start I knew something was wrong. There were noises, footsteps, things moving, lights. Then one afternoon, I came out of my room and there was this thing, like a person, only it was just a shadow of a person, sitting, rocking in my chair by the living room window. I gasped and yelled something like 'My God.' It made this noise so horrible, like a cat in heat, then it stood. I fled my home and ran; I thought I was going to have a heart attack. Anyways, I made such a stink they moved me into the unit I'm in now. Horrible, the whole thing!"

I thanked the lady and we left, heading down to the lobby. I asked if I could get into that unit when the owner returned, and the supervisor said he would try.

Old Haunts and Transient Ghosts
Toronto

I was invited down to a large office complex on King Street, in the financial district of Toronto, to talk with the security staff and have a look around. I was advised that it was a strange place where voices and cold spots followed you around, where odd static and electromagnetic fields (EMFs) came and went without reason, and where staff working overnight were shaken to discover the enormous lobby windows were completely blocked by hundreds of people in old-fashioned clothing, all looking in at them, only to then fade away. It was interesting to note that all the exterior glass in the building was made in Nagasaki.

Frank was a security supervisor of this complex. His responsibility was to ensure the security and safety of all people within the two office towers. He had five staff on his squad who ensured their tasks were fulfilled effectively and efficiently. The buildings were fairly new, and he had worked there from the beginning. The first of the two towers was opened for business and tenants started moving in. From time to time, Frank found himself high up in the building, looking down at the other tower still under construction. He found it amazing that after a few days off, when he returned to work he could see how much progress they had made, adding several floors. After the second building was turned over to the new owners, it was his responsibility to add it to the duty list. It wasn't until the buildings were connected with the subway that the staff started to notice something wasn't right. They all sensed it: there was something there, watching.

It started a few days after the second building opened; there were reports from his patrol staff, building employees, and cleaning staff about wandering smells of freshly brewed coffee and cigar smoke in the executive dining lounge. He spoke to the building engineer, and they thought that maybe the coffee smell was somehow being recycled in the air return system, even though the engineer said that was highly improbable. The cigar smell was another story. There was no smoking within the building, and with the number of smoke detectors on the floor, had someone been smoking, there would have been an activation. These smells would return at odd hours, normally between 3:00 and 4:00 in the morning. There were several high-security areas within the complex, and the executive floors were well protected with state-of-the-art equipment. A control room operator could monitor these areas and know who was on the floor at any given time. Over time, security became accustomed to these roving smells. A patrol officer on that floor would be assaulted by a cloud of cigar smoke, and within seconds it would be gone. The control room operator would confirm that the patrol officer was the only one on the floor. A historical data check was conducted, only to discover that on several occasions no one other than security had been on the floor for more than eight hours.

High turnover of security staff is not out of the ordinary; however, at this location people came and went fairly quickly. Frank admitted he felt unnerved at times, but saw no reason to leave after putting in five years at the site. They moved to night shift on the rotation, and a new hire was brought into the squad. He had passed his orientation training and was now permitted to conduct patrols alone. He was in his late twenties and was experienced, having just arrived from Texas after serving three years with the U.S. Marines. He'd moved to Toronto to marry a local girl. He took his keys and radio and headed out on patrol. His first stop was the third floor, a sensitive computer room. As he got off the elevator and radioed his position to the control room he felt a heavy pressure pushing down on him. He noticed the large plants on the floor start to sway, as if caught in a breeze. He felt uneasy. He called the building engineer to ask if the fresh air supply fans were operating. He was advised that the only system running was the air conditioning units inside the computer room itself. He moved into the hall and placed his hand over the wall vent, but no airflow was coming out. He then turned the corner and looked down towards the access door to the computer room. Without warning a ceiling tile came off the ceiling and hit him squarely in the head. He kicked it down the hall and immediately left the floor.

He arrived in the lobby and told the desk officer to take patrol, because he wasn't doing it! They called the supervisor. After the supervisor heard his explanation they both went up to the third floor.

When they turned towards the hall his face drained of all colour as he saw the ceiling tile leaning neatly against the wall, just below where it had fallen. He yelled at the supervisor, "I kicked that thing down the hall!" The supervisor inspected the tile; it clearly had a boot print on it and there was visible debris from the tile on the floor most of the way down the hall. Everything indicated that the tile did, in fact, get kicked down the hall. Who had brought it back up here and placed it against the wall? They called the control centre. The operator explained that all alarm points indicated that they were the only ones on the floor.

For about a month after that incident, patrol officers on both the afternoon and night shifts reported that in the south stairwell there was always talking on the stairway side of the door. When they would go to investigate, the stairwell door would either be pushed back against them or pulled out of their hand and flung open. No one was ever found in the stairwell.

Frank was on patrol during a quiet night shift around 3:25 a.m. when he stopped to check the executive dining floor. He had forgotten to call the control centre, and the centre put out a call as to the detection of someone on the floor. He called down and corrected his mistake, informing them he was on the floor. As he passed the west side electrical room, he heard a click behind him. As he stopped to listen, the control room called, reporting the west electrical door alarm activation had just been activated. He walked back and found the door slightly ajar. He had just checked that door and it had been closed and locked. He looked inside the small room, which was six feet by six feet, and found no one, then shut the door and checked it again. Locked. As he turned to walk away he heard a click, and before he could turn back, the control centre was calling him again. He closed and locked the door five more times over the next few minutes. The door would remain locked as long as he stood there watching it; however, as soon as he turned to walk away, it would open. It was starting to upset the control room operator.

The building engineer was called to the location. He closed the door and witnessed the problem first-hand. Over the next twenty-five minutes he tested the door — its closure, hinges, latch, handle, and lock — and checked to see if it was level and balanced. He found nothing that would make it open by itself, but every time they went to walk away there was that click. After some discussion, the supervisor, engineer, and control centre operator all agreed that if the door wanted to remain open then that's the way they would leave it.

The complex was attached to the underground and to the subway. By 2:30 a.m. the tunnels were secured and the area and hallways were swept by security to ensure no one remained.

At 4:05 a.m. the control centre alerted the patrol officers and supervisor of a man loitering in the common walkway underground. All three responded to the call. The man, who had shaggy, greying brown hair, a mustache, and a beard and was wearing a heavy, dirty green parka, started to make his way towards the subway access doors. At the last moment he turned into an emergency exit. The control centre called in the new direction of the man, but was unable to explain why the alarm point on the door did not activate. The patrol officer arrived first, followed by the supervisor. As they pushed through the exit the alarm point sounded. They raced down the long concrete corridor to a double alarmed door at the end, which led to the street. They went through the door and the alarm activated. There were no prior alarm activations for these alarms and nowhere for this man to have hidden.

They returned to the control centre and reviewed the surveillance tape; sure enough there he was. The image of him going through the door was just that: the tape showed him passing through the closed door, which explained why the alarm didn't activate. The tape was secured with the security report, collected by management, and never seen again.

On another occasion, the operator called the supervisor to the control centre. The supervisor arrived and was shown some strange phenomena occurring on the sixth floor. They watched the surveillance monitor for a rear hallway on the sixth floor. There were translucent bluish balls of light about the size of a grapefruit coming out of one wall, hovering for a second, then doing a couple of loops and taking off incredibly quickly through the wall across the hall. Sometimes there was only one ball, and other times there were up to three at once.

They called the patrol officer to the control centre. The three of them watched this for several more minutes, then the patrol officer left the room and went up to the floor. He entered the hallway, and although the balls of light were still visible on the monitor, he could not see them. However, he did find a fine line of energy along the path that the balls were flying. He reported that it tickled and caused static, which made his hair stand up and his clothing stick to his body. After a couple of moments he found the axis point to the line and he started to turn in circles, so that only half of his body was inside this static; it seemed comical, as he turned you could see his hair rising and dropping, his clothing being sucked in and let out half at a time, depending on which half of him was in the static field and which half wasn't.

They sent the building engineer to investigate. After a half-hour of him checking the lights and wall plugs up and down the hall and in every office, he looked up at the camera, shrugged his shoulders, and shook his head "No." He could find no explanation.

During the afternoon shift the complex was busy with an army of cleaning staff. During one shift, the cleaning supervisor and the security supervisor were in the elevator, going to check a complaint of garbage in a hallway, when an emergency call came over the radio: a cleaning woman was injured on a lower floor. They reported to the area. When they arrived they found a hysterical cleaner at the door to an office. She wouldn't enter the room. Inside the office was the injured woman, lying unconscious face down on the carpet with her arms at her sides. The security supervisor was checking her vital signs when she came to; she looked around, pushed him away, stood up, and retreated from the room. They went with her down to the lobby, where she sat on a bench and waited for the ambulance to come. The paramedics took her to the hospital. The security supervisor went back up to the floor, checked the room, and interviewed the witness. She was, at the time of the incident, polishing the centre of a long marble table. The table was six feet long, twenty-eight inches wide, and two inches thick, with two marble slabs supporting it at either end, which were twenty-eight inches wide, two inches thick, and thirty inches high. The witness said that as she was cleaning the table, it split across the centre and instead of collapsing opened up like a drawbridge, each piece falling away from itself. The table didn't hit the woman; she just fell in between and stopped moving when she hit the floor. He checked the table and found it strange, as the length and weight should have made the table collapse into itself at the centre. It seemed as if it was pushed from underneath, forcing the pieces to fall in opposite directions.

The woman called from the hospital and requested her friend clean out her locker. She then quit her job, never to return to the complex.

Lights, Camera, Ghosts
Toronto

The renovation of the theatre on Yonge Street was in full swing; it would be returned to its grand old splendour. Security had the task of watching over the site to ensure no unwanted people had access to the building. The security company was caught up in a scheduling nightmare; something was going on at the theatre. None of their staff lasted longer than a few nights, at best. They even tried doubling the guards, which only made things worse as they then had to replace twice as many people. The managers were getting upset, as they were losing well-trained, long-term employees. They were all using the same explanation: "Ghosts."

Officers were reporting chasing noises and fleeting shadows throughout the building, as well as people on the catwalks and in the rooms backstage. It didn't seem to matter how much effort they exerted; these people remained elusive. On the few occasions that they did catch up to them things got really strange.

Mike was an ex-firefighter from Australia. He was a no-nonsense person who didn't believe in any of this ghost gibberish, and thus was quickly assigned the theatre night shift. He reported to work and was given the complete tour of the building by the afternoon staff. He walked them to the door and they started to tell him stories about the theatre. He cut them short and told them he didn't believe in such crap; they just looked at him. As he bid them goodnight he locked the door behind them. The shift ended as it had started, quietly, without incident. The next night he returned and met another crew, who told him that the foreman of the construction company was concerned when his workers came in and found all the rear fire doors wide open. Anyone could have let themselves in and caused damage or stolen supplies or tools. Mike didn't have an explanation, except to say that he knew he had checked those doors every hour and everything was secure. Mike told the other security officer that he last looked at them at 7:30 a.m. and the foreman was on site at 7:44 a.m. There was no one else there. The officer just laughed and said, "Well, must be the ghosts!" Mike walked them to the door and let them out, locking the door behind them. He started his patrol with all the exterior doors, and everything seemed fine. It was at about 4:30 a.m., when he was about to have his lunch, that things started to happen. He had just found a place to eat and laid out his food when he heard a door slam backstage. He jumped up and hurried to see what was going on. He arrived at the door he thought had been slammed and found nothing. He looked around for a few more minutes, then decided to head back to his food. As he turned, he saw a hallway door leading to the change rooms swing closed. Off he went, pushing the door open. He found the light switch and turned on the lights. The door to one of the dressing rooms slammed shut. He pulled out his flashlight and went to the door. As he moved into the room, which was completely empty except for some paint cans, he heard laughter in the hallway behind him. For a moment he couldn't move; he later explained that the laughter was that of several small children. He went into the hall and started to search the building. All night long it seemed that wherever he was, a door would be slammed shut at the opposite side of the building. He never got back to his lunch. That morning as he finished his shift he called in and requested a new assignment. He still insists that his request had nothing to do with ghosts. He just preferred a quieter place for night shift. What could be quieter than a large, empty building in the middle of the night?

It was just after midnight when Sam started his first patrol; he checked the lobby area and made his way through the theatre, heading to the stage, when he heard a noise of metal on metal from above. He looked up above the stage and saw what appeared to be a person standing on the catwalk. He couldn't be sure because the light was extremely poor. He tried shining his flashlight beam up into the tangle of wires, piping, and handrails but that just made more shadows. He called up, demanding to know who was there, but received no response. Then another noise came from the same place. He nervously headed up behind the stage to the access ladder that led to the catwalk. He proceeded slowly and cautiously, the beam of his light acting as his guide. As he reached the top, he looked along the catwalks and felt relieved that no one was there. Then the noise came again. He looked towards the direction of the sound; a man stood there, not twenty feet away — a man who hadn't been there a moment ago. Sam wanted to run but stood his ground. The man, who wore a cap and carpenter coveralls, turned towards Sam, took one step towards him, and vanished. Sam turned and flew down the ladder, heading to the Yonge Street exit. He crashed through the door and out into the street, crossed the road, and used a pay phone to call the company's head office. He reported what had happened and told them to come and relieve him, as he would not go back inside that place again! A patrol supervisor came by and found Sam waiting at the phone booth. The supervisor had to go inside to check the place; Sam refused to go with him. Nothing out of the ordinary was found. Sam was reassigned.

Chris and John were assigned the 4:00 p.m. to midnight shift. As far as the company was concerned they were the two best-suited people for the place, as they were by far the longest lasting security officers to work the site. This shift was their fifth in a row without incident. John was a joker and liked to enjoy himself; all the work was completed and they were just killing time before the night shift came on duty. Chris went to conduct a final check of the rear fire exit doors. John was bored and went up on stage. He decided to take advantage of the acoustical properties of the theatre with an air guitar, starting to sing as if he were performing to a full house. Chris came back around the stage at the floor level, laughing at John. The laughing stopped as Chris noticed a person sitting ten rows back, watching John. Chris started to move forward to see who this person was when he saw a second person two rows behind the first. Chris stopped moving and yelled at John. The two security men looked out into the rows of seats, where both saw a third person further back and to the left. John jumped down off stage, as he honestly thought there was going to be a serious confrontation. Chris raised his flashlight and shone it at the closest of the three, yelling, "How did you get in here!" As the light hit the person, the person vanished. The two officers moved up the aisle, and the other two intruders disappeared as well. They thought that perhaps they had ducked down and were hiding.

The night officer arrived, and the three officers searched the entire place for almost two hours, finding no one. All the doors were as Chris had last seen them — secure.

The Replay
Toronto

George and Mary moved into a socially assisted building in Regent Park on Sumach Street. George was on disability and proceeding with physiotherapy, and Mary worked part-time for a local hospital. The building was in poor condition but would have to do until they were able to get back on their feet financially. The apartment was a fair-sized two-bedroom that had been freshly painted, although the walls were rough from filled-in holes and large cracks. The eat-in kitchen was large but dingy with no windows, and the front door had three deadbolts, two of which had no keys.

Mary felt that there was something wrong with the apartment the first day they moved in. She couldn't identify what made her feel that way, she just felt uneasy about it. George tried to console her, putting her anxiety down to their immediate situation and reassuring her that things would get better soon. Mary had to rush off to work on the afternoon shift and George did what he could by unpacking items that he was able to lift without assistance. He wanted to have most of the place in order by the time Mary came home from work. George thought he had unpacked some glassware and put it in the china cabinet, but there it sat still in the box; he decided maybe he was feeling the stress of everything as well. Then he noticed the coffee mugs he knew he had unpacked sitting in a box beside him. He distinctly remembered taking those mugs into the kitchen. George leaned forward on his chair and looked around the room, wondering what was going on. He was beginning to have his own feelings of uneasiness.

Mary arrived home from a long afternoon shift at the hospital and found that George had gone to bed. She retrieved a glass of milk from the fridge and looked the place over to see the progress of unpacking; it seemed that George had completed quite a lot. She turned on the television and fiddled with the aerial, trying to capture a station. A local channel came half into view, the sound was perfect, and the picture faded in and out of snow. She curled up on the couch trying to unwind from her day, her thoughts skipping between the events at the hospital and her situation at home. She was about to get up and have a cigarette when she heard water running in the bathroom. She remained seated, believing that George had gotten up and would be out in a moment. The water shut off, but George didn't appear. Then the back bedroom door slammed, so hard that it rattled the apartment. She jumped up and started down the hall when George came to the door of their bedroom. Their eyes met, and he was the first to speak. "What the hell was that?" he asked.

"The back bedroom door!" she stated, looking down the hall at the closed door.

George took the lead, with Mary following close behind. He threw open the door and switched on the light. Nothing. Mary checked the windows, but they were all locked.

"Maybe it was from upstairs," George offered. Neither really believed that explanation, but neither wanted to discuss it.

The next week was quiet as they started to settle into their new apartment; the last of the boxes were finally gone, and the place was looking more like home. Then the alarm clock in the bedroom started to go off every night at 2:45 a.m. They couldn't explain why, even after both George and Mary inspected the clock. George said it must have been getting old and malfunctioning. They had to put up with the unscheduled disturbances until the following payday when they went out and bought a new alarm clock. Mary unceremoniously tossed the old clock down the garbage shoot. That night they were awakened by the alarm at 2:45. Mary started screaming at the clock — lack of sleep and stress seemed to be catching up with her. George just leaned up on one arm and looked at her from his side of the bed. She finally lay down and they drifted off to sleep. From that moment on the clock no longer did anything unusual, and the 2:45 alarms stopped.

One day soon after, Mary got up early and went into work for the day shift; George got up an hour later and prepared for a trip to the therapist. He stepped into the shower, drawing the curtain closed, and as he did so a shadow of a person crossed the curtain. George paused with fear, then threw the curtain open. No one was there. He stepped from the shower, reached over, and locked the bathroom door; the uneasy feeling was back.

Later that evening at dinner George told Mary what had happened. Mary, with an unexpected calm, said, "We have to move."

"We can't afford to right now!"

"We have to do something; I never said anything to you but I've seen the shadows in the bathroom too."

George just looked at her; they sat quietly and ate their meal.

As time went on they both heard odd noises, things moved or went missing, and shadows were seen in the bathroom. They stopped talking about it, and Mary started leaving earlier to shower at work. George felt powerless, as though he had let Mary down. If he could only get back to work they could leave this place. Tension was building between them.

George helped a friend fix his computer, and when he was finished his friend handed him one hundred dollars. He didn't want to take the money, but the friend, knowing George's situation, insisted. George reluctantly accepted. He took the money and went to the grocery store, where he had an idea. George rushed home and started cooking a romantic dinner complete with wine, candles, and flowers.

When Mary arrived home from work she was ecstatic. They ate and talked and enjoyed each other's company; it had been a long time since he had seen his wife laugh. He let her sit and relax with a cigarette while he cleared the table. A low noise came from the living room. Mary noticed it first. She asked George if he heard it, so he stopped and listened. The horrible sound grew louder, like steel scraping jagged rock. George went out into the living room, and the sound was louder. He went over to the couch and put his head near the wall. Mary followed. "It's right there!" he told her.

Terror was on her face. "That's our bedroom wall!" she whispered. The sound stopped abruptly. They listened closer and thought they heard a female sob, then the water started in the bathroom. They moved to the hall, standing there, fear holding them in place. The water shut off and the back bedroom door slammed shut. They wanted to run from that place, but they didn't; neither could explain why they just stood there, looking down that hallway at the back bedroom door. The light had come on and they watched as shadows moved in the light at the bottom of the door. George started to go down the hall, but Mary grabbed at him, pulling him back. She jumped for the phone and called 911. Six minutes later there were two burly police officers at their front door. The apartment was searched and nothing out of the ordinary was discovered. Mary thought the officers were understanding, George thought they were considering taking them to the psychiatric hospital. They made an application to move, using the excuse that the unit was too large for the two of them and that it would suit a bigger family.

George started to talk to people in the neighbourhood about the history of his apartment unit. A long-time resident mentioned that he thought a woman had been murdered there in the early 1980s, but he wasn't absolutely sure if it was his unit or the one above his.

It was a long five months, but the transfer came in and they were situated in a new apartment, just across the courtyard from their old building.

Interview on Reincarnation
Toronto

I met Michael at work; he had just started as a summer student, having finished his second year at university. One morning I noticed Michael looked pale; I asked him if he was feeling okay. He told me that he would be fine, it was just a headache. Later that afternoon he mentioned to me that he gets these headaches from time to time. Then for some reason he started telling me what comes with the headaches; he called them visions. The stories were interesting, but what I found strange was that he really didn't talk much to anyone at work, and he definitely wouldn't have had any idea of my interest in the paranormal, but it was me he sought out to relay some of his stories.

He sat in class, his head starting to hurt, the type of hurt that meant an episode was about to commence. He was becoming used to it, and he just sat there, rubbing his temples, looking through blurry eyes. The class ended and he saw the teacher at the front of the room, talking with several students. He gathered his books and rose to leave. As he moved between the rows of chairs, he saw something that drew his attention, another woman standing behind the teacher. Two things drew his attention to her: she had a glow to her, and she was older than the students, although not as old as the teacher, who was in her early thirties. He made his way up to the front of the class and stood beside the woman. He seemed to ask her what she was doing there, without speaking aloud. She looked at him and replied, "Waiting to be born!" He looked at the teacher, interrupting her conversation, and asked, "Are you pregnant?" She became angry at the personal question, and after a few words he was sent off to the office. A few months later she started to show, and a few months after that the teacher was off on maternity leave.

We talked about the reports that we have read in countless publications, where unseen forces have attacked expectant mothers, inflicting injuries on their stomachs, such as scratches and bite marks. If Michael's vision was correct, is this the method in which reincarnation occurs? Does the soul, hovering near a prospective mother, wait for the right moment to enter and thus be reincarnated? If this were the case, what would happen if the soul destined to be that new child was forced aside by a transient spirit at the moment it was required to enter, losing its opportunity to be reincarnated? Could the attacks be out of anger and frustration aimed at the transient spirit and not the prospective mother at all?

Of course this is all speculation; what Michael's vision means remains unknown.

A Dedicated Worker
Mississauga

Prior to the government moving into the warehouse near Eglinton Avenue it had been a small automotive manufacturing plant. A woman in her early twenties died there in a tragic accident, and most people who have stayed overnight in the building maintain she is still there.

Security and surveillance personnel protected the facility twenty-four hours a day, and technicians would, on occasion, work overnight. The facility had the latest state-of-the-art electronic security equipment.

When the sun went down and everyone went home for the evening she would start to wander the building, tripping alarms, opening and slamming doors, and turning on the equipment lying around. Most people on the night shift had seen the black shadows that moved quickly from the women's bathroom across the open warehouse to the offices thirty feet away.

A corner of the warehouse was the hot spot for activity. Loud sounds of steel banging on steel would emanate from this corner of the building, even though the area was clear of any material. A few minutes after the banging loud talking would start. Security would investigate, even though it was clear from the surveillance cameras there was nothing there, and each time security approached the area everything grew quiet. Phantom doors that no longer existed in the facility would be slammed shut. Each time security would go on alert and there would be more alarms from the main office.

All security personnel and several management members viewed an extremely impressive surveillance video. The tape was recorded on an exterior camera that was mounted on the corner of the building overlooking a main access door, a parking lot, and a vacant field beyond. It was late, 3:41 a.m. as recorded on the tape. A very strange movement caught the surveillance officer's eye. Imagine a clear container, fashioned to look like a human body, then filled with swirling white smoke. The form moved from the field to the building at a steady pace, crossing the parking lot. The operator called his partner to have a look at what he was seeing. He wanted confirmation that he was, in fact, seeing this. His partner moved in and looked at the screen, his eyes transfixed on the thing outside. It shifted direction slightly and headed towards the brick wall. The wall, at one time, had an employee entrance door, which had been removed and bricked over. As it neared the wall, approximately three feet away, the whole thing swirled and rolled into a tumbling fog and passed through the wall, disappearing from camera view.

The surveillance personnel couldn't believe their eyes and reviewed the tape over and over again that night. In the morning they showed it to their relief staff and management. They made a request to copy the tape, which was denied due to the fact that it was a government facility; permission could not be granted to copy a surveillance tape that may or may not show any portion of the protective measures of the building. The tape is most likely in a storage box at this time. I fear where the tape may end up after three years, the prescribed duration for holding tapes by this branch of government.

It was about 1:10 in the morning; Joan, an executive assistant, was working late trying to tie up loose ends of a large project that was nearing completion. She came out of her office, waved at security at their post, and headed off to the women's washroom. Joan was an efficient, no-nonsense woman who did whatever it took to get the job done. As she entered the stall she lit a cigarette, which she felt would cut her break time in half. As she did so, she heard the bathroom door open and someone enter the stall next to hers. She thought this was strange because she wasn't aware that any other females were working in the building this late. She stated that she was having a quick smoke and that she hoped it wouldn't bother them. A woman replied, "No, I know how it is, these breaks go so quickly!" Joan came out of the stall, curious about who was working so late. She came out of the bathroom and stood there, waiting. She didn't know the voice, and she knew everyone who worked there. The security officer walked over to say hello, and Joan asked who else was working. The officer ran through all the names, and she was the only woman working at the time. Joan told the officer that there was a woman in the bathroom, maybe someone they had missed. He became slightly defensive, stating that no one had been missed. Joan went back into the washroom, only to find it empty.

The Jumper
Toronto

Sometimes strange things happen while on the way to an investigation. I had an interview with a group of security personnel in an old building on Bay Street, in the financial district of Toronto. They had reported some unexplained occurrences and offered me the chance to have a look. I exited off the Gardiner Expressway and worked my way up Bay Street. It was a lovely summer night, with hardly any humidity. It was nearing 12:30 a.m., yet there were still pedestrians walking the street, some coming out of local pubs and others just casually strolling, looking in the shop windows.

I had just passed King Street and was driving in the curb lane when I noticed a man on the sidewalk. He was near the curb ahead, and it appeared that he was waiting to cross the road. The first thing that grabbed my attention was that the man was wearing a three-quarter-length black coat, not suitable for the weather. Before I could think any more about it, as I was just about to drive past him, he stepped off the curb, directly into the path of my car. I slammed on the brakes, hard. With less than four feet or so to stop, I knew hitting him was unavoidable. I wanted to pull the car to the left, but couldn't, as this would have put me into the side of another car and put them into oncoming traffic. I swerved slightly and my car stopped, bringing on a torrent of blasting horns. I got out and moved to the front of my vehicle, finding nothing there. Two people across the street looked at me like I was nuts, and at that moment I had to agree with them. I was sure that he was there and that I had hit him. I looked under the car again — still nothing. I just shook my head in wonder, stood up, and turned around, almost bumping into a woman at the curb who was looking under my car as well. I had to ask, "What are you looking for?"

She looked up at me, shock on her face, and replied, "The man you just ran over!" So there it was, a person who had seen him as well — what a relief! I asked her what she had seen and she described him exactly as I had seen him, long coat and all. Now, realizing I hadn't hurt anyone, we shook off the anxiety by laughing in that moment of uneasiness, then said our goodbyes. I continued on to my appointment, albeit a little slower.

Who's Haunting This Building?
Toronto

Near the intersection of King and Bay streets sits a grand old building, built around 1934. It houses several large corporations and a working population of around four thousand people. The company that originally occupied the building is now gone but maintains two floors within the building, one for storage and one for the original boardroom. When you emerge from the elevator it's as if you have stepped into a bygone era. The floor that contains the boardroom is like a time capsule from the 1930s. Its richly polished, ornate cherry wood panelling, grand crystal chandeliers, and solid twenty-eight-chair table, which runs the length of the room, show wealth and power. Used on rare occasions for special meetings and the odd movie shoot, mostly it sits vacant — with the exception of an unseen presence that roams the floor.

Security patrols the building and must tour this floor several times each shift. They will tell you strange stories of experiences they have had throughout the building, particularly on that floor. There are many debates over who roams the floor. Some believe the CEO, who once commanded the head chair of that spectacular table, still lingers there. Others think it may be Harvey, a security guard who was assigned the front reception of the floor in the 1940s, still on the job. Others feel it could be a maintenance man named Frank, who in 1951 fell off a ladder while changing lights and struck the table, breaking his neck.

The reports started to surface in the late 1970s (in the previous decades, professional businesspeople did not discuss such things). There are many stories of pipe and cigar smoke appearing from nowhere then disappearing in a moment. A source never seems to be found.

One officer on the night shift, while conducting his patrol, entered the floor from the south stairway. As he did so he instantly felt a deep sadness, an emotion he couldn't explain. A moment before he had been in a great mood, speaking to his duty partner at the security desk. The floor also felt colder than the other floors. He started across the floor, and as he proceeded he heard heavy footsteps on the hardwood floor behind him. He stopped and turned to see who it was, but no one was there. He waited a minute then continued on his way, again hearing the footsteps behind him. He headed for the north stairway and the footsteps quickened, growing closer, louder. Then something pushed past him, cold. He felt the goosebumps grow on his flesh and he grabbed for the door handle, pushing it open, eager to get off the floor. As he did so, a door on the floor closed, near the private meeting rooms. He didn't look back; he just kept going all the way down to the lobby and his partner at the security desk.

Jeff, another security officer, is considered the resident paranormal guy. He collects stories about the building from his colleagues. He admits that all that goes on in the wee hours of the morning intrigues him. He took me over and showed me one elevator that is different from all the others. "This is the original car, an executive express to the boardroom floor, and when they retrofitted the building the owners wanted to keep it original." It had all the splendour of the floor it serviced, with rich cherry panelling, beveled mirrors, and ornate chrome decorations. As we stood there discussing the elevator, the doors closed and it took off, up to the boardroom floor. I looked at him, and he smiled. "It does that all the time; we have reported it to the elevator technician and he says it only runs when it's called. A year ago we added an extra security measure, which included this car. After business hours we toggle a switch at the security desk, which places all the elevators on lockdown. This means you can call an elevator to a floor, it will pick up the person, and the computer control brings the car straight down, no stopping along the way. This elevator will go to the boardroom floor, then stop two floors above that floor and come back down."

"Why two floors above?" I asked.

"Back in the thirties that floor was the original executive offices," he responded. A moment later the elevator returned to the lobby, where it sat quietly for the rest of the night.

We toured the floor, and Jeff told me about how several security personnel requested transfers after experiencing things on this floor. They would get to the middle of a room and the lights would turn off on them, even though the light switch was in view. The worst incident happened to a trainee, who on her first night was touring the floor.

Every time she reached for a door handle the door would fly open on its own. She finally stationed herself in the lobby and refused to go anywhere in the building. That was the first and last time he had ever seen her, as she quit the next morning. Then there was the time a film crew was working on the floor. It was a big film production; they had twenty-six battery packs for their cameras, and all the batteries died at once. They were very upset. The sound crew kept hearing whispers.

He pointed out an office behind reception, and we headed over to it. "This is where everyone hears the talking."

"Talking?" I asked him.

"Loud whispers, you can never tell what they are saying, and as soon as you get to the door it stops."

He admits the sound of someone walking, following you around the floor, is very creepy, but insists his curiosity keeps him here. I reminded him what curiosity did to the cat. He didn't laugh. As we headed to the elevator we heard a door close; we just looked at each other and boarded the elevator.

The Old Woman Who Never Left
Toronto

A large house stands on a hill on Jones Avenue, overlooking the road below; built in the late 1920s, it has been renovated several times throughout its history.

Agnes lost her husband after fifty-three years of marriage. Her only other relative was a daughter, now living in the U.S., which made things difficult for her. It was 1970; Agnes had renovated the house and moved into the attic, leaving the home open for renters to help make ends meet. She passed from this life in her sleep at the age of seventy-seven, up in that attic. Her daughter finally returned home to sell the house. The place was sold two more times over the next four years and is now being rented out again.

The Randle family thought it was perfect for them, paid their first and last months' rent, and moved in. Eric, sixteen, was the eldest son and was looking for privacy; he was immediately drawn to the attic apartment. After brief negotiations with his parents, which included his accepting responsibility for putting out the garbage and keeping the garage clean, he was awarded the small apartment. He couldn't have been happier.

Eric set up his room and settled in nicely. The first night he had what he described as the best sleep he could remember. However, the second night things changed. The light outside the room hanging in the stairway turned off by itself and the floor by the door to the room creaked, as if someone was moving there. An access door, four feet high and thirty-two inches wide, led to the rest of the attic, which was simply insulation and empty space. Even though there was an eye and hook latch on this door it slowly swung open in the middle of the night. This went on for several nights. He mentioned it to his mother, who explained to him that it takes time to get used to new places and that strange sounds were to be expected. This didn't make Eric feel any better, so he installed a slide bolt lock on the door, and it seemed he had at least solved the door problem. As for the light turning on and the noises, they persisted.

His parents started to notice strange things on the main floor of the house. Things were being moved, things went missing, and all the kitchen cabinet doors were found wide open in the morning. Several times they found the stove elements turned on and candles lit on the kitchen table.

One of the strangest incidents, according to Mrs. Randle, involved the basement door. For some reason it had an old heavy-duty eye and hook latch on the basement side of the door. One day she went to go down to do some laundry and found the door latched. She banged on the door, wondering who was down there and why the door was locked. Although she heard someone moving around down there, they wouldn't answer. She started to grow angry and called for her husband. They considered their options: there were no other ways into the basement, and the previous owner had installed security bars on all the lower windows. Left without options Mr. Randle took a step back and kicked the door. The door pushed against the heavy bolt, and he could see through the open door's edge that he had bent it. Again he kicked it, and this time the bolt ripped out of the wood. They went down the stairs, ready to read the riot act to whoever was down there. The basement was empty.

The family started to hear walking on the stairs — slow, deliberate footfalls starting from the main floor, continuing all the way up to the attic. Each time someone came out of his or her room to see who was on the stairs, the sound would stop and not continue until they went back into their room. Once, Eric's twelve-year-old sister, Sandra, came out to see who it was and decided to put it to the test. She sat down in the hall and waited for almost forty minutes. Finally giving up, she went back into her room, and the walking immediately started up again.

The small door in Eric's room started to open up by itself again, regardless of the slide bolt. Each night he would ensure it was locked, and every morning it would be open. Eric was finally fed up with this door, so he pulled his dresser in front of it. Early the next morning, while Eric was sleeping, he felt something cold close to his face. He stirred and opened his eyes, screaming with fright as a face looked back at his, only a few inches away. An old woman's face, with wild grey hair. He sprang up and backed into the wall, and the image vanished. A second later he watched the small door swing closed; his dresser had been pushed aside. He flew from the bed and ran downstairs, waking everyone in the house. Eric refused to go back upstairs; he wanted to leave the house and never come back. His parents tried to comfort him, without any luck. Eric slept on the couch for a while and moved in with a friend a week later.

The family finally got out of the lease, moving out a few months later, and were reunited with Eric.

Is it possible that Agnes still wanders the house, retreating to the attic, away from her renters? Did she wonder why this boy was intruding into her space?

Undying Love
Peterborough

A young married couple, Eric and Lori, dreamed of owning a vacation property. They both had full-time jobs and worked hard all week long. They longed to find a quiet escape, away from the city. Eric had fond memories of spending time at his uncle's cottage on Buckhorn Lake as a boy and really loved the area, so they focused their search in and around the Kawarthas.

There were such a variety of wonderful cottages for sale that they felt it would be only a matter of time before they found one perfect for them. It was, unfortunately, poor timing on their parts; the interest rate was the lowest it had been in years and the housing market was on fire. Those who didn't buy a home invested in cottage property, causing the prices to go through the roof.

After two summers of searching, they came to the disheartening conclusion that they just couldn't afford to buy. At this time Lori's friend told her about a wonderful trailer park. Lori and Eric discussed this previously unexplored option. Eric was somewhat doubtful that he would like being in a trailer park as he had heard awful things about them — they were too crowded, no privacy, not enough trees, and it just wasn't a cottage. Still, Eric promised to keep an open mind and agreed to go have a look.

They drove out and met with the park owners, who showed them a variety of trailers for sale. Eric came away impressed with the park. It was next to Pigeon Lake, the lots were large and well treed, it wasn't overcrowded, and there was plenty of green space throughout. They talked about one trailer in particular that they had seen; they both thought it was perfect. It was on an extra-large lot with more than a dozen mature trees and had a grand deck. The master bedroom was large enough to handle a king-sized bed. It had air conditioning for the summer, a forced air furnace for those cool fall nights, and the price seemed low. Eric's skeptical mind started working. He came right out and asked the park owner, "So what is wrong with that trailer?"

The park owner explained that there was nothing wrong with the trailer; the trailer's owners were a retired couple, the wife had recently died, and the husband just couldn't face coming up anymore. It was a sad story.

After some deliberation they agreed to buy it. The very next weekend they took possession and moved in. They spent all day cleaning and setting up their things. They pulled the dining room table and chairs out of the trailer's living room and placed them in the sunroom, opening up a great deal of space inside the trailer and allowing the sunroom to be better utilized. That evening, while sitting on the deck having a cool drink, Eric had to admit he really liked it. He smiled at Lori and they both looked on as their dog explored the lawn; in the distance they heard the loon calls over the lake.

That night Eric was woken up at 3:00 a.m. by the sounds of walking in the kitchen. He rose on one elbow and listened. It was distinctive footfalls on the floor, either in the kitchen or living room. Lori lay sleeping beside him. He desperately tried to equate the sounds to his dog, and then to his amazement he heard a cupboard door snap shut. Eric knew that unless the dog had recently developed opposable thumbs, something else was causing the sounds. He got out of bed and almost stepped on the dog, who was lying tight against the bed looking towards the kitchen, as if hiding. Eric went to the hallway and turned on the bathroom light. He could see into the kitchen and some of the living room; there was nothing there. He walked into the living room and turned on the lights, noting that a kitchen cupboard door over the stove now hung wide open. He slid the glass door to the sunroom open and crossed the room to make sure the outside door was locked, which it was. Finding nothing, Eric went back to bed, making it a point to leave the bathroom light on.

The next few weekends the sounds persisted, waking them and leading them on futile searches. One day a neighbour from the next site over came by to ask Eric what was going on at his trailer. Eric told him he didn't know what he meant. The neighbour explained that he had seen lights go on and off inside the trailer, and what was really creepy was that he heard heavy footsteps on the deck and the sliding glass door open and close. He looked right at Eric and said, "You guys weren't up, no one was there!"

Eric turned and looked at the trailer and wondered what they had gotten themselves into.

By the end of June the sounds had finally stopped; the uneasy feelings gave way to fun in the sun, barbecues, campfires, and good company.

The next season, during the May long weekend, the activity started all over again. This time it was more terrifying. It was late, they had retired to bed, and everything was quiet. Around 3:00 a.m. Eric woke to footsteps in the kitchen, heavier this time. Lori was still asleep, but she was tossing and turning. She was also speaking in her sleep, something Eric had never heard her do before. She was whispering yes and no answers. Then the walking came up the hall towards the bedroom, accompanied by the menacing black shadow of a person on the wall. Eric thought his heart would stop beating. All of a sudden the dog dove onto the bed and darted to the edge facing the hall, snarling and growling at the doorway, seemingly ready to defend them against whatever lurked there beyond that shadow. To Eric's amazement the shadow backed away from the bedroom. The dog lay down on the bed and stared down the hall, which had now gone silent. Lori went quiet, and he wondered how she could have possibly slept through all this. Eric just lay there and listened; the dog finally put her head down, still focused on the hall. Eric waited for more; it never came, and he finally fell asleep.

In the morning Eric told Lori about what had happened. She remembered dreaming about talking to a lady in the trailer, but couldn't remember any specific details.

The sounds continued, although they were no longer menacing, until the end of June.

The ghostly visitations didn't return the third season. Eric's explanation was that the husband had passed on, and he believes that the two were reunited and have moved on together.

A View into the Past
Sunridge

Built in the 1850s, the four-bedroom house sits atop a hill, overlooking the picturesque view of Lake Bernard. The small, dusty town rarely receives visitors, with the exception of those seeking a deal at one of the large car lots, all of which seem out of place. At one time the main highway ran through the centre of town, but in recent times it has been moved, now bypassing the town completely. The phrase "Blink and you'll miss it" has never held more truth.

The house has remained in the same family from the day it was built to the present. Unfortunately, either there was no activity in the house or it was not reported until strange things were noted in the early 1970s. A second home was built not far from the original in order to supply the owner's family with all the modern conveniences. The original house was left open for out-of-town relatives to visit during summer vacations. It was during these times that strange things were noticed.

The place was fairly large, open, and inviting. Inviting during the day, that is, but when the sun went down at night, there came an uneasy feeling for the men. They would report oppressive feelings of being watched, making them feel unwelcome. Some of the men would turn away from the comfort of the four large bedrooms available and sleep out in their cars. The same feelings did not seem to afflict the women in the house.

Could the original owner be unhappy about the use of the home? Could he be trying to convey that information, along with his judgment, across the boundary of life and death? He lived in a time when the church spelled out all the family morals; in their strict teachings the people of the day had clearly defined rules of right and wrong. As the house became a vacation spot, there were, on occasion, late-night card games, drinking, and carrying on. Most couples weren't married but nonetheless shared a bedroom.

This was one of those times. A group of people sat around the large dining room table, playing poker and drinking. The youngest of the group, who were not permitted to participate, sat in the living room, talking. The living room was large, with a sofa, three chairs, a coffee table, and several tall glass cabinets.

During the conversation, the girl who sat in one of the chairs near the far corner by the window stopped talking. The boy looked at her and immediately thought that she didn't look well. Her skin was pale and her eyes were glazed over. He leaned forward from his seat on the couch, about to ask her if she was all right, when she raised her hand in front of her face in an attempt to grab something. She spoke, asking where the smoke was coming from. He asked her, "What smoke?"

"The smoke right here in front of me." He looked from several angles but could not see anything. She stiffened in her seat and told him that the room was funny, changing. "The smoke is from a pipe, right here, and I see a low table with candles on it … two candles, they cast a glow off the wall." He got up and went to the place where she was pointing. Nothing but a large glass cabinet filled with books stood against the wall. "And over there, against that wall, I see a bed. A single metal frame bed." He looked, but only saw two large chairs there. "And on the bed, a brilliant white light. It wants to fill the room." He didn't know what to make of any of this and it was starting to scare him. Another girl, Kate, who was in the dining room, got up and headed down the hall to the stairs heading up to the second floor to get something. As she passed the open door to the living room the girl turned and, in a voice the boy didn't recognize, demanded that Kate not go up there. Kate, without question, turned and went back to the dining room and sat down. That's when the boy grabbed the girl and shook her. She fell back into the chair and looked strangely at him. She had no recollection of what had just occurred. The boy recorded the events on a pad of paper.

The next morning when the boy saw his aunt, he asked her if he could speak with her in the living room. He told his aunt that something weird had happened the previous night. He asked her about the history of the house, the layout of the living room, and the pipe smoke. She confirmed the low table and the chair her husband's father used to sit in to smoke his pipe. She stated, "Over there is where he slept when he got sick, so he could be close to the washroom." He took all the information in and handed her the paper that he had made the previous night. She couldn't believe it. She looked up at him and in a quiet voice said, "The place where the bed was, is where he died."

The Cabin in the Woods
Sudbury region

There is a cabin in the woods just northwest of the small northern town of Levack, Ontario, just off Highway 144. The locals believe it was built as a hunting retreat, but no one knows who owned it or when it was built. Even Ed, who at the age of ninety-six is probably the oldest living resident in the town, says the cabin was old when he was a child. He remembers seeing it with his father when they used to hunt rabbits outside of town. His father warned him to never go near it. Ed has many strange stories of the place. I asked him if he'd listened to his father's warning. Ed just laughed. "I was a kid, as soon as he told me that, he had my curiosity on high." He stopped laughing and looked at me, now with seriousness. "I should have heeded his words."

Ed and his friends Henry and Walter wandered out there one afternoon to have a look around. They entered the cabin, which was just one large room with a cast-iron stove in the centre. There were a couple of old tables, a cot, some shelves with old dusty bottles, and, on one table, tin pans and a cooking pot. Walter found a chewing tobacco tin. They searched the room for anything of interest. The door slammed, startling them; they all turned to look at the door, and Henry started to move towards it when a black shadow came from the corner of the room and blocked it. Henry jumped back.

The shadow was like a black mist in the shape of a large man. They all panicked. Walter was the first to dive out the window on the opposite side of the cabin, and Ed was right behind him. Ed hit the ground running, but Henry didn't come out. They didn't know what to do; they were kids and were terrified. They stood there yelling for Henry to come out, but he didn't.

A few minutes passed and they debated if they should go back in and get Henry or if they should go and get help. They decided to go back in, so they ran around to the front of the cabin and crept up to the front door. They paused there, listening, but heard nothing from inside. Ed reached out a trembling hand and grasped the door handle, took a deep breath, and pushed, letting the door swing open and bang against the table inside. They jumped back again. They called for Henry, but there was no answer.

Walter inched into the doorway; Ed was so close to him they kept bumping into each other. They entered and looked around, thinking that maybe Henry had escaped, and then they saw him in the far corner sitting on the floor. They rushed over to him; he was trembling and breathing funny, staring at the door. They grabbed him and pulled him to his feet, yelling at him, but he never spoke a word. They left the cabin and pulled Henry along as they ran back to town.

Henry never talked about what happened in that cabin, and he wasn't permitted to chum around with Walter or Ed anymore. Ed thought it was at the end of that summer that Henry and his family moved to Quebec. That was the last he ever saw of him, and whatever happened to him in that cabin remained his secret.

My brother and some men were hunting out that way when they came across the cabin, finding it shrouded in a fog that appeared nowhere else. People report strange lights and sounds out there, and strange things move in those woods — things that are best left alone. The funny thing is, if you are brave enough to go out there today, you will not find a single piece of graffiti on that structure. The local kids all know it's there and no one will ever go out there to do what kids tend to do.

A mining company purchased the land about twenty-five years ago. Security has on occasion driven by and checked this place. I've talked to some of the guys, and they hate going out there. Steve, a security man, said the place is extremely disturbed; birds and crickets don't make a sound in that part of the woods, and you always feel as if you're being watched.

Now these stories piqued my curiosity, so I drove out to the cabin with a friend who lived in the area. He told me that it was a bad idea for us to go up to the cabin. I reserved judgment.

We pulled off the road and prepared to walk the rest of the way. It was a beautiful summer day — the sun was high in the sky and the mercury was pushing 27° Celsius. We entered the woods and walked for about twenty minutes. I instinctively knew we had arrived before my friend said anything. The nature sounds had stopped and the forest had become cold. We stopped and looked at the cabin from a distance for some time; neither of us spoke. My friend finally broke the silence. "You going up there?"

"Yes, are you coming?"

"No, I'll wait here!"

So there it was, if I wanted to have a look I'd be on my own. I walked towards the cabin and it seemed to be growing colder. I arrived at the door and paused, looking both ways along the face of the structure, then looking back to make sure my friend was still waiting. As I pushed the door, it arched open and something hit me. It was an overpowering feeling that I needed to leave this place, that I shouldn't be here. I took a step forward into the open doorway and then turned and walked away back to where my friend stood.

He looked at me. "So?"

"You're right, this place should be left alone!" I told him, looking back at the cabin. I thought he was going to laugh and tell me "I told you so" when the door slammed shut. The sound was loud and startling and we turned in defence. We headed back to the car, the hot summer sun, and the sound of birds singing.

The Investigations

After reviewing the surveillance tapes an old saying came to mind: "I wish these walls could talk, what stories they would tell!" And here I was, tape in hand, having just heard past events, conversations, and things that … scared me!

The Haunted Schoolhouse
Pickering

I met with Paul and John; we loaded the equipment into the car and began our journey to the site. The location was an old schoolhouse near Pickering, Ontario, built in 1875 and now being used as a community centre. The centre has had numerous reports of strange occurrences dating back to at least the 1960s. The Hauntings Research Group, who had invited us to join their continuing investigation, had previously investigated the site. We were all to meet there by 4:00 p.m.

The Hauntings Research Group is a group of dedicated professional paranormal investigators based in Peterborough County that I found on my quest to discover associates with whom to share ideas and theories. I was very impressed with them, as they take nothing for granted. They make no claims, and as the majority of their group are true believers, they face each new piece of information they have collected with a balanced skepticism. I truly believe there isn't anywhere they would not go to find the proof they, like so many of us, seek. The group was founded by Dee Freedman and Anita Goodrich, both of whom conduct investigations and are psychic sensitive. Krystal Leigh, a field investigator, is psychic sensitive as well.

We pulled into the parking area, where the rest of the team was already unloading equipment near the front of the building. As I was exiting the car I noticed that John was showing interest in a storage shed. I grabbed my 35-millimetre camera and headed over to where he was standing. As I was walking up to him, I checked the camera's built-in light meter and set the shutter speed and aperture. As soon as I reached where John was standing, the camera's batteries died. These had all just recently been replaced. The interesting thing was that not only the meter and control battery but also the flash and power winder batteries were dead, a total of eight batteries in all. At about the same time Krystal entered the building and was loading the film into her 35-millimetre camera, when her batteries died as well.

Both Anita and Krystal reported a heavy feeling upon entering the main hall, which would have been the original schoolhouse section of the building. A video camera was set up at an exterior gate leading to a marshy bog on the property line to the rear of the school. In the previous investigations conducted by the Hauntings Research Group, this gated area was the scene of paranormal activity.

Upon her arrival Dee picked up on a name coming to her out of the blue, like so much of this information does: "Beth" or "Bertha." This name would stick with her until she could figure out why she had received it.

She went into the building, placed her bag down in the kitchen, and began wandering the interior, trying to vibe it out. As she did so, the group began taking dimensional measurements of the inside of the original schoolhouse, so they could set up video surveillance in the optimum locations. Dee took a temperature reading, which was 66.6° Fahrenheit (19.2° Celsius).

Dee placed toys around the main hall, each one centred on an X of blue tape. Dee then found some old framed historic photos of students and teachers in the far corner. There, she was drawn to an Elizabeth, who in 1888 was a teacher at this school. She also found a Bertha, who had been a teacher as well; however, she had a deeper connection with Elizabeth.

John, Paul, and I went past the gate and stood there for a few minutes. John felt that something had taken place there. He sensed that sometime in the past a group of people had used this spot to conduct some sort of ritual that involved killing animals. Pigs were a specific image that he received, and possibly a person was killed as well. He pointed out the circle, which was well defined by the trees. The limbs on the trees within this circle seemed to be weighted and pulled downward towards the ground, something the trees outside the circle did not exhibit. The energy within the spot was heavy, negative. In the very centre of the circle was the gate. There seemed to be a message from nature itself not to pass the gate: the tree limbs bent like elephant trunks low to the ground, forming a natural barrier to the gate. There was also a large pine that had fallen onto the property, blocking a portion of the gate. John felt that whatever these people had done had opened a vortex or doorway, and something had come through, something that had never been physical. He didn't want to call it demonic, as he felt it was more mischievous in nature. Whatever this thing was, it fed off fear, and the more innocent its victim, the better the meal. This was a disturbing revelation because of the proximity to the schoolhouse.

It was starting to get cold, and the sun was fading fast. Everyone had the opportunity to have a good look around the property and inside the building. I was getting gauss meter readings off the scale near the fence line and gate area, readings I didn't understand. There were no power lines or other sources of electrical energy, but I was getting readings two inches off the ground, then nothing until I reached five feet and higher. As strange as it was, I had to dismiss it as possibly due to high solar flare activity we were experiencing.

Paul and Krystal met me at the gate. As we stood there talking, we picked up on a noise from beyond the fence. Paul and I went into the forest, trying to follow it; we traversed bog holes and fallen trees about three hundred feet out. Krystal called from the yard, "It's moving this way, along the fence line." We circled around and headed in towards the fence, trying to catch up to whatever it was. The going was slow as we sought a path with our flashlights. As we neared the gate, Paul, who was in the lead, stopped abruptly. I caught up to him. He just looked at me for a moment, then pushed ahead. When we arrived at the opening by the gate he looked at me again and told me that as he was nearing the circle, something hit him in the centre of his chest. He described it as if someone had put a hand out to hold him back. It was brief and then it was gone.

Dee noticed small lights moving amongst the trees, which she described as resembling fireflies. We were fairly sure there were no fireflies so late in November, especially with a temperature of -1° Celsius. Others were reporting strange light phenomena around the property; lights that would dart in and out of the trees, standing still and then moving at various speeds. I moved to the edge of the building, looking towards the gate, while the others went to the entrance of the driveway. I caught a glimpse of a very bright flash of light at the fence line, about three inches off the ground, next to the fallen pine. I checked with Krystal, as she had equipment in that area. There was nothing set up that would have produced such a flash of light. We all ended up down by the gate again. Krystal had goosebumps and felt she was being watched, as did I. She felt safe only within the group and didn't want to venture off by herself.

The lights kept moving in and out of the trees, circling the property, disappearing, then reappearing behind us. I had a feeling about it, but I didn't realize I had spoken aloud until I received acknowledgement from Dee, who was standing beside me. It was like an animal circling its prey, looking for a vulnerable side.

I hadn't seen Anita go into the forest, but I saw her emerge through the gate on her way back to the yard. She reported feelings of disorientation when walking past the gate and into the opening of the forest, a phenomenon that had been reported often over the years.

Dee pointed out the full moon hanging low in the sky: the lunar eclipse had just begun, adding to the eeriness of this place.

There was a Mini Mag-lite with the lens removed turned on and affixed to the gate. The light, running on two AA batteries, should not have surged; however, everyone saw this light intensify like a lighthouse beacon for almost two minutes, then return to normal.

Paul wanted to go back into the forest, Anita agreed to go with him, and they walked past the gate. The rest of us stood on both sides of the gate and watched their flashlight beams move deeper into the heart of the trees. The light beams disappeared, as if they had moved beyond a solid wall of blackness. Dee called Paul on the two-way radio and had a difficult time as we were faced with a heavy static, static that hadn't been there a few minutes before. We called out several times, until we heard a "We're okay" in return.

There were noises in the trees above their heads. They searched for animals with their flashlights but found none, yet the noises persisted. Anita fired her digital camera up into the trees. Paul spotted something at ground level and had to pause, unsure of what he was looking at. "What the hell is that?" he said, aiming his flashlight beam at it. Anita looked at it, and they both realized that what they were looking at was a human head lying on the ground under several fallen trees. They pushed aside their fear and tried to get in closer. They couldn't see a body, just the head: eyes and lips black, mouth crooked, face leathery. Anita took several photos of the scene. Then orange lights came up out of the trees, drawing their attention, like eyes floating. It was hard to tell because of the distance and elevation, but they felt they were probably nine to twelve feet in the air. They followed the lights with their flashlights until they disappeared behind a tree. They looked back to the head and it was gone. That was enough for them, they quickly made their way back to the gate and the rest of the group.

They explained what had happened and what they had seen. Of course, with such a story, they were faced with skepticism until Anita displayed the photos on her digital camera's review screen. The image of the head was clear. We headed inside the building to seek much-needed warmth. We discussed what this image could mean. Was it a warning? Was it a psychic image, indicating a body was there? Was it something else? We wanted to go back out there to dig in that spot. Someone produced a shovel. Several of us went back into the forest, right back to that spot, and conducted a search of the area. We found that it would be impossible to dig, due to the way the trees had fallen. Several trees were intertwined, and the way they were lying wouldn't allow for the swing of a shovel. They would have to be cut away first. We agreed to mark the spot and come back when we had all the right tools to conduct a more thorough investigation of that piece of ground.

We walked back to the yard; the eclipse was full and it looked as if there was blood on the moon. We went back inside to warm up.

John, Paul, and I assembled in the entry hall. I didn't invite the rest of the group for two reasons. First, they had conducted investigative work here and I didn't want them to influence John. Second, I wanted to keep them separate so I could compare notes on what John picked up to what Dee, Anita, and Krystal had put together.

John began using his pendulum. "Are there any spirits here that wish to communicate?"

A yes, indicated by the pendulum.

"We wish to know, when you were physical, were you a student at this school?"

[No response.]

"Did you attend here?"

Yes.

"Do you have any contact with what is outside beyond the gate?"

No.

"Are you aware of what goes on out there?"

[No response.]

"You know to stay away from there?"

[Fear.] Yes.

John stopped. "What is in here is completely separate from what goes on out there." He went on, "I get a strong impression of a maintenance man, I want to call him a caretaker, in the area of that outbuilding, the shed, or a structure that stood there previously. Is this correct?"

Yes.

"You are the caretaker?"

Yes.

"You watch over the children here?"

Yes.

"You make sure that no one crosses over into that area, is this correct?"

Yes.

Directed at us: "He is a caretaker in every sense of the word!" John continued, "You knew about that area even before your death?"

Yes.

"Whoever this maintenance, caretaker man was, he knew or very strongly suspected about what went on in that part of the property by the gate. He returned here because he knew there would be influence over the children. He is very much involved here! Joseph! I want to call him Joseph! What we have are energies of children in here, he hovers in this area because he realizes there is a very serious danger involved for these children. He believes in this, and what could happen."

John paused.

"He died from a cut, tetanus, a problem with his blood, some sort of infection. He came back because he was aware … 1920s. Some confusion … he either heard of something going on, or had first-hand knowledge of what was going on here."

[Pause.]

"He heard and saw things when he was alive, whatever is out there tried to exert pressure over him to bring the children into the circle beyond the gate.

"Hungarian or Lithuanian is his background, he has a distinct accent!

"Joseph … pronounced 'Yosef' … was very clairvoyant, very quiet and humble. He truly cared for the children very much. At the moment of his death he realized he couldn't go, he had to return and stay here to protect the children!

"The circle is still there, it is made up of spiritual energy. What lives out there has free run, but it's like a lion in a cage, it needs people to bring it what it needs. Its power is from the circle, as it moves away from the centre it loses its power. It is inhuman, never physical. Will not use the term demonic to describe it, although it can be very malevolent and mischievous. It is old, powerful, clever, and lonely. It is the way it is simply because that is its nature, it has no moral sense of right or wrong!

"Joseph was a spiritual man, he knew what was going on here.

"The image that I get is 1917/1918, influenza killed a lot of people in the area, like it did everywhere. A lot of fathers, uncles, and brothers were away at war, Joseph felt as if he were a surrogate father figure to a lot of these children!"

John stopped.

We sat with the rest of the group and discussed the collected information. Dee and Anita had picked up, for the most part, the same information that John had. Dee added a last name to Joseph, which she felt was something like Heirnan.

For what it was worth, we had collaboration from three sensitive people, all of whom had picked up the same information from the site separately.

The investigation unfortunately drew to an end. The events of the evening were both intriguing and frightening. We all wished we had more time to spend on this strange patch of ground. As for whatever is out there in the forest, just beyond the gate, we are comforted in the knowledge that Joseph the caretaker will be watching and protecting those souls that still linger within this very old schoolhouse.

A Call for Help
Oakville

It was a Monday morning when the phone rang. It was a woman named Diane; she wanted to know if I was the guy who investigated paranormal phenomena. She had gotten my number through another company as a referral. After I assured her of who I was, she went into her story. I stopped her and told her I would call her back. I wanted to prepare myself and to confirm her phone number. She agreed.

Later that day I called her and conducted a preliminary interview over the phone, which lasted about forty minutes. She told me that she runs a house as a museum, which is used by school groups to learn about life in the 1860s. The staff dress in period costumes and run the house as it would have been run in that era. The problem was that there seemed to be activity taking place in the building; the most disturbing of all was a ghostly woman who would appear to children from time to time, sending them screaming off the porch and into the field beyond. She really wanted some help. I set up a date when I could assemble my team and ensured that she was available as well.

Two weeks later at 7:20 p.m., we arrived at Diane's office and met with her. I introduced Paul and John. She wanted to tell us more about what was going on, but I stopped her because John was present. I didn't want him to know anything about the place or what was going on. I wanted him to vibe it out and report what he was picking up on. She led us outside and we followed her car a distance to the house. As we were nearing the house, John was staring out the window of Paul's car. He told Paul to slow down for a moment, then he looked back at me and said, "There is a young boy in the field by the road. He died there, an accident ... an apple cart overturned and crushed his leg. This field was an orchard at one time and he was badly hurt in the accident and died from infection not long after. But he is still here." We drove on, towards the house.

We arrived at the house at 7:45 p.m. The night was overcast and raining, 17° Celsius. The house was a two-storey wood structure built in the 1840s. There was no electricity. We grabbed the flashlights, and

Diane gave us a full tour of the building. As we toured the house, there were the odd sounds of something moving around, always one room away from our location. The main floor of the house consisted of the kitchen pantry, dining room, parlour, and an unused back bedroom. A second floor contained two children's rooms, the master bedroom, and two common areas, one of which was a sitting area, the other probably meant for a baby's crib. There was no basement, just a small dirt hole under the kitchen. We finished the tour and went outside to the cars. Diane was going back to her office. She asked us to lock up when we were done and see her before we left. I agreed, and she drove away. We retrieved our equipment from the car trunk and went to the kitchen. As Paul and I prepared the equipment John walked around the main floor, trying to get a feel for the place. He was drawn to the parlour, stopping in front of a large oil portrait, one of several that hung on the walls. This one was of a woman. He looked at the portrait for a couple of minutes, then said, "It's you. This is your house and you are still here, aren't you?" He looked at us. "We should work in this room!" he said, moving across the room to sit down. We agreed.

As John settled in, Paul and I started to map the house. Paul was taking control photos and I was recording various instrument readings from every location. The first indication of possible contact was on the second floor, at the opening to the first child's bedroom. It was two degrees lower than the house temperature, which was 16.2° Celsius. I also picked up a fleeting electromagnetic field of 7 milligauss. Then the reading went to 0. I scanned the room and found it near the back corner, then it was gone again. I went out into the hall and picked it up in the second child's bedroom. It seemed to retreat to the back of the room, and then it was gone. I went to the common area, and there I lost it altogether. I scanned the rest of the floor, but was unable to pick up on further anomalous readings. The room temperature had returned to normal, without variation. The signals I had received seemed to follow a retreating pattern, sweeping a very narrow path, going through every room on the upper floor, then vanishing. Paul had finished taking the control photos, and we were ready to go downstairs to join John in the parlour. Paul placed a tape recorder on the upper floor stair landing and set it to record.

I turned on my tape recorder; John was going to attempt to establish communication. He was going to use a pendulum, which would give yes or no answers, and he was going to attempt to tune into any energy psychically. The questions, as well as any information in an answer, would be spoken aloud by John for the benefit of our records.

"Is there a spirit in this house who wishes to communicate?"

Yes!

"Do you live in this house?"

Yes.

"You are a woman!"

Yes.

"You are the mother of many children in this house!" John paused and smiled.

How dare you come into my house uninvited, you wretched, evil …!

"Would it be fair to say you are angry at us?"

[No response.]

"We wish you no harm, we are all here as friends! Do you wish to harm us?"

No! Despicable heathens, get out of my house!

John looked at us and made a face. "I don't think she likes us!" He continued his questions. "Do you know what year it is?"

Yes.

"Is it 2002?"

Why are you being silly?

"Is it 1902?"

Are you disturbed?

"I'm sorry, I'm not very bright. Is it the nineteenth century?"

Yes, stupid boy!

John laughed. "Do you know a person named Terry, Terrance?"

Terrance is a boy.

"Poor Terrance left here, didn't he?"

A flood of information hit John: Yes. That little boy was only seven years old. How could he leave me? I can't leave him alone, I'm taking care of his room!

"You are very, very angry because your home has been moved away from his grave?"

Yes!

"She stays very close and hopes that all the little children who come here will encourage her son/grandson to come back. Every so often one of the children that visit the house will remind her of Terrance or the little girl that used to play with him, and those would be the ones she attempts to communicate with. In her excitement she would be right there in front of them, wanting to grab them, hug them."

"Do you know where Terrance is buried?"

Yes, but I can't go there!

"This boy died of some sort of lung disease, TB, scarlet fever. These people were Irish, they came from Ireland … and she is very unhappy!" John paused. "There is a bond with a Laura, and also with a Mary. She doesn't want anyone in here … Confusion … No adults, but the children, the adults bring the children. The children are her hope and also her frustration."

John stopped and took a break.

Paul went upstairs to retrieve the tape recorder, stopping halfway up and signalling to me. There was a sound above on the floor, then a movement, a flash of white crossing the common area, passing through open space where there was no floor above, and then disappearing. He aimed the camera at the spot. We looked at each other and said the same thing: it looked like a nightgown. We checked the photo … nothing. We retrieved the tape and came back down to the main floor, going into the kitchen.

John wandered in and looked at us. "She is very hesitant about giving us her name."

I asked him if we should try to get her to spell out any information that she wanted us to know. John stated that she couldn't spell, it would only add to her frustration. John headed back to the parlour and sat.

"Am I speaking to Laura?"

Yes.

"Do you like the children who come here?"

Yes.

"Do you wish they could stay?"

Yes.

"Laura is not your name, why are you using that name?"

No response.

John paused, looking over his shoulder. "She is very upset, nobody wipes their shoes before coming into the house … no respect!" He turned his back to us. "I am looking at a painting on the wall [referring to a portrait of an older woman in the parlour]. Is this a painting of you? Are you the woman who roams this house?"

Yes.

"Is there anything we can do for you?"

Yes, leave!

"Are you alone in this house?"

Wait until my broth— husband gets home!

"Your husband has been gone a long time, is this true?"

Yes.

"Is the year 1823?"

Yes.

"You lived in the United States before coming here?"

Yes.

"Pennsylvania?"

Yes.

"Your family was involved in mining?"

Yes.

"Someone in your family made a lot of money?"

Yes.

"Is your family name Logan?"

No.

"It is Lucas!"

Yes. If I give you something to eat will you leave?

John laughed.

We took a break.

Paul and I went outside to look around the property. John was left alone in the parlour. While outside, both Paul and I observed a small white orb floating near John. This was seen through the window at about ten feet away. We took a photo, then moved in to get a closer look. I looked behind us to see if there might be a source of light casting a reflection. The field was black and there was no moon. At about three feet from the window the orb vanished. We went back inside and told

John about the orb. He said she was very close by, but he wasn't aware of any light in the room with him. The photo was inspected and nothing out of the ordinary was noted on it.

"Please leave the children alone, you are just scaring them. If you can do this we will do everything we can to help you. Do you understand?" John said to the spirit. He turned to us. "She gets it!"

John said he had everything he needed and thought we were done, and Paul and I agreed. We packed up the equipment and loaded the car, then locked the house and drove back to Diane's office. We met with Diane and discussed some of the problems that we thought were the main causes of the haunting.

John explained, "She was a pillar of the church. The children would read to her, they would read her the Bible. A man died in that unused bedroom on the main floor, off the parlour. There were three infant deaths, either stillbirths or death of the child within a single day. She was a frigid person, regarding sex as being for procreation only. Other than that she would insist that her husband slept somewhere else. The woman was a definite control person, this was, without question, her house! She is upset about the roses, they are not right! Are there roses at the house?"

"Yes, in the back!" Diane stated.

"You may want to let the groundskeeper look at them, see what the problem is. A mat should be placed at the door; have everyone wipe their feet before entering. Please use some respect at the house. There is a smoking pipe in the master bedroom, this really bothers her. It seemed to suggest that the room was used in a partnership, and that smoking was permitted in the house. Neither is true, you have to remove the pipe!" John then asked, "Who are Laura and Mary?"

"Mary and Laura work for me, they operate and clean the house. How do you know about them?" Diane said.

"I picked up on them in the house. There is a strong bond between them and the spirit. I'm a little concerned about it, but it's nothing I can put my finger on. The house was moved to this location. Is that correct?"

"Yes."

"Well, you left a grave behind, a seven-year-old boy named Terrance. There was some confusion as to who he was, but I understand now. He was her grandson, her daughter died when he was very young, so she raised him like a son. We might want to locate the grave at the old site and see if we can relocate it here. Do you think we can do that?"

"I have to try to confirm this information first, I'll get back to you on that."

John filled her in on the family history and other information he had received. He also mentioned the boy and the apple cart on the way to the house. We said our goodbyes and left the location, heading for home.

A week later I contacted Diane and she was completely amazed. She had gone through her archives and discovered that John had been 100 percent accurate on all the information he had presented her about the family, the house, and their history. Even the information about the orchard and the accident was correct.

She also stated that the roses had been growing wild over the roof of the house, so they had been trimmed back, and that they had followed all of our other recommendations.

I made a follow-up call two months after our visit and discovered that not a single incident had occurred since. All was completely quiet. She told us that there is no record of a grave at the original site, but that didn't mean it wasn't there. They would be more than happy to move the grave to the house if we could locate it. We agreed, and will investigate this in the near future.

The Coach House Haunting
Mississauga

Frank and Joan were moving out. They'd had enough of unexplained noises, lights that turned on and off by themselves, and doors that swung open, aided by unseen hands.

They lived atop a large coach house, built in 1910. From outside, the place looked small and cramped, but as you climbed the stairs to the raised patio and entered the front door, you were instantly aware of that deception. With a full bathroom, eat-in kitchen, three bedrooms, extra-wide living room, and fifty-foot storage room, there was plenty of space for a medium-sized family.

Paul and I arrived and interviewed Frank first. Although he loved the place, he was tired of the unexplained things going on — shadows that moved down the hall, items that disappeared. Joan talked about the storage room door, which opened by itself, and noises in the storage room. She took us up to have a look. The door was heavy and solid with a working doorknob and latch. Paul tested the door and the hallway floor but couldn't manage to get the door to swing open without physically pulling it open. We went inside the cavernous storage room and inspected the interior. We couldn't find any sign of mice, birds, or other animals to explain the noises. There were no windows or vents in the area. The couple told us that even though they were moving, they would have possession of the property for a few weeks more, and if we wanted to continue investigating the coach house, we were free to do so.

Paul and I met with John. As usual we didn't brief John on the reported phenomena. We arrived at the property and met Frank, who told us all their possessions were out of the house; with that he gave us a copy of the key, telling us to lock up when we were done.

The three of us climbed the stairs to the front door. Paul opened the door and let John enter first. We toured the interior; I noticed John eyeing the storage room door briefly then moving on down the hall, passing the bedrooms to the living room. For the first twenty minutes John just wandered, getting a feel for the place, going into every room.

He finally joined us and said we should set up in the living room. We broke out the equipment and set up a small table and chair. I took several control photos, and Paul set the tape recorders.

John settled in and let out a large sigh, looking around. He began, "This is a place of service and toil; a lot of infighting, childlike behaviour, gambling, fighting, fooling around, gossip, backbiting, stealing. There seem to be many different levels of time."

He stopped and tried to refocus. "Early forties, I see a woman cry, another who has lost her baby … A bad boss, tough guy, hot tempered, don't cross him. A lot of heartache in this house in these years … this was not a happy household. Much restriction, heartache.

"Whatever was going on in this house ended in 1945. In 1946, someone new came in, took the destiny of this place and manifested it in new directions; a new era of toil … a lot of darkness was uncovered here. Many things were discovered and re-hidden.

"Depression, suicide, restriction, secrets, many secrets … the energy does not flow well in here. They hang around, spiritually unaware; they see what they want to see, more of the earth plane, not tuned into what is good for them on a spiritual level. They are caught between death and life.

"There are spirits here, there is one that is particularly aggressive, almost to the point of being compulsive, again restrictive, stuck here, in a way by their own choice. Not wanting to see that they could move on, very secretive, communicates in a subversive way, very depressed. If they could cry … this one cries. Very unhappy here."

John pauses, Paul changes the tapes, and I take of couple of photos down the hall, towards the storage room.

John starts again. "One lusts for money and power over what he once had. He wants it in his hand, demands power, grasping, greedy, jealous of the physical reality. If he could, he would like to inhabit a physical body … that much want. Sexual feelings, lust, power. The owner [Joan] probably had erotic dreams here, brought on as a manifestation of this spirit. Very lonely.

"Cover-up, murder for money … opposite of family, it was all about breaking up family, the destruction of a union. Unclear.

"They move through the entire spectrum of emotions. A lot of money passed through this place. Poverty of spirit, very sick. I don't like it here ... I don't like it. It's a place of disturbance, spirits argue here, they fight here."

He paused.

"A suicide, very depressed, he sits there by the window. [He indicates the window behind me. I take a photo of the area.] Stares out the window for hours on end, smoking cigarettes."

We took a break and wandered about the house, leaving the tapes running. Then we returned to the living room. John prepared, taking out his pendulum. "Is there a spirit present in this house that wishes to communicate with us?"

Yes.

"Do you mind us being here?"

No.

"Were you once physical?"

Yes.

"Did you live here when you were physical?"

No.

"Did you visit this place frequently?"

Yes.

"Is this your place now?"

Yes.

John paused. "They want us to leave. Do you want us to leave?" There was a pause before the response.

No. [Lonely.]

"Do you miss Frank?"

[No response.]

"Do you miss Joan?"

Yes. (This time an audible voice said, "Yes." It was heard by all three of us and captured on the tape recorder.)

"Were you fond of Joan?"

Yes.

"Do you want them to come back?"

Yes.

"This place has been sold, there will be a new family with children moving in soon, will this be okay?"

No. [Pouting.]

"Did you die here?"

Yes.

"Were you a child when you died?"

Yes.

"It's a girl, a little girl! You're a girl?"

Yes.

"You used to play here?"

Yes.

There was an interruption, something banging on the patio by the front door. The three of us went to investigate. We ended up on the outside patio, but all was quiet.

When we returned, the storage room door, which had been closed and latched, was open. We closed the door and then attempted to do everything to get it to open again, including opening the front door and jumping up and down in the hall. It wouldn't budge. We went back into the front room.

"Are you still here?"

Yes.

"Was that you who opened up that door?"

Yes.

"Do you play in there?"

Yes.

"Is there something secret about that room?"

Yes.

"Something hidden in that room?"

Yes.

"Would it be okay if we looked in that room?

Yes.

"Will you show us where to look?"

Yes.

"Something you want us to know about that room?"

Yes.

"Sometimes you hide in there?"

Yes.

"Something scary happen in there?"

Yes.

"Were you put in there when you misbehaved?"

Yes.

"Locked in?"

Yes.

"Not allowed to come out?"

No.

"But it's okay now, you are allowed to join us in the living room! Do you like that we are here?"

Yes.

"Are you nine years old, you were nine years old?"

Yes.

Cold air passed between us, lasting a few seconds.

"When did you die?"

1919.

"Did you know the man who built and owned this house, Mr. Black?"

Yes.

"You used to play with Mr. Black's children?"

Yes.

"Played with the dolls here?"

Yes.

"Played hide-and-go-seek?"

Yes.

"That's a fun game?"

Yes.

"You got sick, you couldn't come here anymore?"

Yes.

"Your tummy got sick?"

Yes.

We heard a whimper in the corner of the room.

"Did you die in this house?"

No.

"Did you come to this house after you died, because it was so much fun here?"

Yes.

"Mr. Black was good to you?"

Yes.

"Do you know the Blacks are no longer here?"

Yes.

"Friends here with you?"

Some.

"Do you live far from here?"

No.

"Did your mommy work here?"

No.

"Your father work … it was your uncle, your uncle worked here?"

Yes.

"Your uncle would bring you here?"

Yes.

There was the sound of movement down the empty hall, then nothing more.

We inspected the storage room and the rest of the house again. We entered the carriage house below, and after some climbing around we found a walled-up stairway that would have led up to the closet of the coach house. It was walled at both ends and well hidden.

We could understand why the stairway was walled in, but John didn't think it was relevant to the haunting, it was just one of the many secrets hidden there. He felt that over the years several people worked, lived, and died in this coach house; a few were decent, hard-working people, but the rest were corrupt and foul. They would steal from their boss and from each other. There was a great deal of violence here — fights, attacks on women, and child abuse. He didn't really want to go back inside. We collected our equipment, locked up, and returned the key. It was interesting to note that Joan confirmed the dreams she had while living there. She wouldn't elaborate, she just said that they were extremely sexual.

Lost: The Family Secret
Mississauga

Paul and I were to meet up with Joe, the business manager, to discuss the investigation and to have a look around. We arrived and checked the main floor. The building had been a large private home in the 1850s, after which it was converted into a business; it is now being used as a pub. It consists of a large bar, a dining area, and a kitchen upstairs, with bathrooms, an office, and a storage area down in the basement. Joe took us downstairs; next to the washrooms he told us how the workers and patrons reported extreme cold spots and uneasy feelings there. Next to the phone in that area was a small closet. When Joe opened it a high quantity of positively charged ions were detected briefly. We moved on to a secret room, which was fifteen degrees colder than the rest of the basement. Joe stopped to tell us about some of the incidents, and I couldn't help but notice a chalkboard near the washroom. Written on the board was, "Shhh, please do not disturb our resident ghost, Minerva!" Joe said that a patron who claimed to be psychic told him that the ghost's name was Minerva.

We followed Joe up to the main floor, where he told us that glasses and ashtrays would fly off the bar. People would report their hair being pulled or touched and complain of feeling cold. He then told us that he had been scratched on the back of his neck in one encounter. In another encounter, an employee was going out the back door of the kitchen to have a smoke when he saw a female standing there looking at him. He had to take us to show us because it was difficult to describe. When I saw it I understood. The outer door was a solid wood door, which opened out to the deck. The inner door was a screen door, which opened into the kitchen. When the screen door was open, it was against the kitchen wall. When the employee saw the spirit she was between the wall and the screen door, which was fully open. The space between this door and wall is less than three inches. The incident was brief. Another situation involved a different employee, who was fearful of changing in the locker rooms because of feelings of being watched and uneasiness. He had decided to change into his work clothes in the hall outside the locker room. It was on this occasion that he witnessed a transparent apparition of a girl walking down the hall towards him. As she neared him she disappeared through a solid door into a storage area.

Our clairvoyant, John, had arrived and entered the main door to the pub and went straight to work wandering the main floor, trying to pick up on psychic impressions. Another team member, John M., met up with Paul and I, and we set out to place our equipment in the basement. Paul had some good ideas as to where to locate the cameras so I left them and went back upstairs, where I placed an infrared camera in the kitchen, reported to be one of the heavily active spots. Paul and John M. placed a camera in the common hallway outside the lower level washroom, which was reported to be the most active place in the building. The unit being used was a wireless camera with built-in microphones so Paul could monitor any activity from the main floor entrance. A tape recorder was then set up in the secret room.

John M. and I started taking meter readings and photos in a crisscross pattern throughout the main floor. We found one area, close to the far side of the bar, which held a few strange anomalies. We found an electromagnetic field reading in mid-air of 7 milligauss (it was 5 feet from the floor, 4.5 feet from the ceiling, 3 feet from the wall, and 3 feet from the bar). The reading seemed to exist in an eight-by-ten-inch space. There was also the presence of charged particles and static electricity. The frequency counter picked up 4 Hz, then started to climb — 7 Hz, 14 Hz, 27 Hz. Then the reading went to 4 Hz before disappearing completely, at which point all equipment readings were zero. We could find no reasonable explanation for these readings or their sudden disappearance.

A few minutes later, Paul reported seeing a large shadow on the camera. It came from the closet and headed off towards a steel door by the men's washroom.

We met up with John on the main floor near the stairs. He said, "It's a girl, nineteen. She has some sort of illness, hunched over, hard to breathe. Mentally challenged. Her arms flail around, hard to control. Almost seems like she has multiple sclerosis. Very disturbed. Let me get this.

"Ah, she becomes confused when people call her Minerva or Mini; that was her aunt's name. When people here call out those names she thinks her aunt has come back and goes off looking for her. Each time brings disappointment. This is actually cruel, it gets her upset and frustrated. It's been going on for a long time.

"She spends most of her time in the basement, and I get this image that she travels from the far end of the basement under the bar to the kitchen." He looked at Joe. "Is there a tunnel?" Joe did not answer.

John paused for a moment. "Wow, this is really complicated. Her Aunt Mini is actually her grandmother. Mini's daughter got pregnant ... 1890, out of wedlock. This became the family's secret. The family was very important here, very affluent. This could have been scandalous. While she was giving birth Mini's daughter died, and the baby had very serious medical problems. The child was kept, even though they felt she was an embarrassment to the family. She was kept in the basement in the secret room. She wasn't allowed outside or permitted to play with any of the other children. Hidden away!"

He headed for the stairs to the basement, stopping on the midway landing. "There was an uncle, a creepy guy who would fondle her and make advances towards her." We continued down to the basement.

At this point all of the surveillance equipment in the kitchen stopped operating without any reason. The footage taken with the other camera in the basement was missing the first half-hour, during the same time period that the other equipment malfunctioned. However, on the tape in the hidden room, Paul had captured noises of things moving around and then a very clear voice of a girl saying, "Mommy!"

John stood in the hall between the closet and the washrooms, trying to tune into what may have been going on in the basement. He turned and looked at the chalkboard. Looking back at Joe he said, "It's all here, you don't need me to tell you what you already know!" Pointing to the chalkboard he read it aloud. "Shhh, please do not disturb our resident ghost!" He rubbed the name Minerva out. "You wrote it yourself, she doesn't want the attention, or to communicate, just to be left alone." He wandered off to a steel door. "Where does this go?"

Joe said, "You can open it, it goes to the office and storage." It also led to a back stairway up to the kitchen.

John looked at us. "This is the tunnel I felt was down here. This is how she gets from that room up to the kitchen."

He stopped near the change room and sat down on a box, looking at me as I sat near him and turned on the tape recorder. He was already picking up information from her in his mind. John took out his pendulum, trying to focus the communication with her.

"We are here as friends, no one will hurt you. I'm sorry for the disruption, is there anything we can do to help you?"

Yes.

"Are you afraid? Hmmm! Are you scared?"

Yes.

"Nothing to be scared of! Do you have a safe place here … a safe place down here?" He turned to us. "She doesn't understand." He continued, "Ah, you have a baby! A little dolly."

Yes.

"The baby is with you."

Yes.

"Pretty baby, she has nice hair."

Yes.

"Do you have a friend that plays with you?"

No, my friend died. My friend died. My friend died … No one to play with. [Fear.]

"Nothing to be scared of! Do you like all the people that come here?"

No.

"Do you want the people talking to you?"

No.

"Are you allowed upstairs? Can you go upstairs?" He paused. "She doesn't understand." He asked a series of questions. "Do you know your name? Do you remember your name? Do you remember what they call you? Can I ask your name?"

Yes.

There was a long pause before John's next question. "Is your name Minerva, Mini?"

NO! [Upset, stomping on the floor.]

John paused. "But you know Aunt Mini?"

Yes!

"Are you having trouble breathing where you are?"

Yes. [Scared.]

"Nothing to be scared about." John paused briefly. "Do you play with the children upstairs?"

Yes. [Timid.]

"It's all right to play with the children, it's okay!"

Yes.

"When you go up there I want you to look out the window. Can you look out the window?"

No.

"It is okay to look out the window."

No.

"It's safe, look out, that is outside! Outside!"

Yes. Horses?

"Yes, the horses are outside. Can you do that please, there is no need to be down here, it is better for you upstairs."

Yes.

"At the window."

Yes.

"What is your name?"

Bet, Bet, Bet ... Beth ... Beth! [Speech impediment.]

"Your name is Beth?"

Yes.

"Elizabeth?"

Yes.

"Thank you."

John paused for a moment. "She is very confused and scared. She doesn't want the attention she is getting and it is cruel to be calling her aunt's name out loud. She needs to move on. She is drawn to your wife, Joe, and I suspect that you may remind her of someone, someone she didn't like. She lived and died down here, and when she died nobody noticed for a day or two. It was her medical condition, she couldn't breathe. At first I thought there was a fire because she was extremely hot and suffocated. I see now it was part of her condition and a fever. She was nineteen but with an undeveloped mind. She was drawn to hair, especially blonde. She had this uncontrollable urge to touch it, feel the softness, but because of her condition she would lose control of her muscle co-ordination and instead of stroking the person's hair she would inadvertently give it a tug. She meant no harm to the person, of course. She is the resident entity here. There are others that will drop in occasionally. There is a man, a son of Minerva, who died in the war in 1914 and I believe he is buried in a cemetery close by. The people who owned this home had a lot to do with this town, a lot of power and influence. Elizabeth was one of their secrets."

We headed upstairs; it was 5:00 a.m. and time to pack up. As we disassembled and packed the equipment John gave Joe his advice: he should simply stop enticing this spirit, no contact should be attempted whatsoever.

It was funny, after all the equipment was safely loaded into the car and we were all saying our goodbyes, loud noises started in the kitchen. I walked over, pushed the door open, and peered in. Nothing — at least nothing that I could see.

The House of Secrets
Toronto

It was a two-storey semi-detached home, built around 1898 in the Bloor and Dufferin area of the city. It was rumoured that a small-time bank robber had owned the home in the 1920s, and upon his arrest none of the money was ever recovered. People in the community speculated that the money was hidden somewhere in the house. Although there were several historical searches we could not substantiate this claim. However, starting in the mid-1930s right up to the mid-1960s there were constant break and enters at this house, though nothing was ever taken. The break and enters have been confirmed as fact.

The owner was an elderly lady who had become ill. She was living alone in the house, and her nephew would drop by on a regular basis to help her and do her shopping for her. She was brought to stay with family until she was feeling better.

The house was old and becoming rundown and it was decided that it was the perfect time to do some renovation work. Her four nephews felt that they could do most of the work, but some of the more difficult jobs, such as plumbing and electrical, would be left to the professionals.

The contractors arrived and were met and let in by one of the boys. They quickly went to work on the upstairs bathroom. One of the jobs required them to run a new drainpipe from the upper floor to the basement. As they worked, alone in the house, they started to notice odd sounds that put them on edge. When one had to go into the basement and the other had to remain on the upper floor it was the last straw for them, as their tools kept moving, doors kept closing, and the sounds grew louder. The workers abandoned the job and fled the house.

The boys went in to do some drywall and painting. One brought a tape recorder along in his toolbox. As they stopped to have a break, he placed the tape recorder upstairs and pushed "record," then they all went outside for some air.

Later, he retrieved the tape, tossed it in his box, and finished the work. A few days later, when he had time, he listened to the tape and found voices on it, voices that were very distinguishable. He let the others listen to the tape, and sure enough, they all agreed that the voices were of their deceased grandfather, uncle, and cousin.

The house required further renovations in 2004, and two of her nephews took an interest in completing the job. Paul was the one who had the knowledge and expertise to do most of it. Mike would help him where he could. As a result, Paul ended up being in the house alone for long periods of time. It was during these times that things would occur. Most were subtle noises, normally in a distant part of the house, away from where he was working. Sometimes the noises were too close for comfort and the remodelling work would become almost impossible. As any contractor will tell you, you cannot comfortably hang drywall by yourself and watch your back at the same time.

Paul was working on the upper floor, in the front bedroom. He was on the ladder, applying a base coat of paint to the new walls and ceiling, when he heard something come down the hall and into the room. It seemed to be moving quickly, and before he could react, whatever it was slammed into the ladder without warning. The ladder shuddered from the impact and the paint flew everywhere. It was gone as quickly as it had come, leaving him with quite a mess to clean up.

It was finally time to go after a long but satisfying day's work. He had accomplished a great deal. As he started down the stairs, he noticed a shadow of a person on the stairwell wall pass him, going the opposite way up the stairs. He stood there, confused for a moment, and looked around to see if he could find a logical explanation for what he had seen. He couldn't. With that, he headed out the door and went home.

On another day, Paul was working in the house alone. He heard the odd noises, which he had become accustomed to. He went upstairs and made his way down to the rear bedroom. As he was standing there, he heard it. He froze, heart pounding. There was deliberate walking in the middle room, the floor creaking from constant movement on the floor. For a moment he wasn't sure what to do. He was trapped — the only way out was the stairs, which were past the middle room. He listened, and the walking continued. He moved slowly up the hall to the middle room; its door stood wide open. He paused, then turned to look inside that room. The floor continued to creak in small circles. Then it stopped. He stepped into the room, and the temperature was freezing, at least twenty degrees colder than the rest of the floor. He had no explanation for this, as all the windows were closed and the furnace was working. About an hour later he returned to the room and it was just as warm as the rest of the house.

We decided that this house would be perfect to conduct an investigation: it had the history, there seemed to be activity, and it was empty. We went to the owner and asked for permission to conduct an investigation. During our visit we talked about the house and some of the things that had happened there.

It started in the early 1960s, when the family had arrived home from a visit at a relative's home. When they came in the door their four-year-old son immediately ran up the stairs, heading to the washroom. The parents went into the living room, where there were other relatives waiting for their arrival.

As the boy made his way down the long hall to the bathroom, his Uncle Lou came out of the back bedroom and smiled at him. Lou patted the boy on the head as he normally did and told him he was a good boy. He then headed for the stairs and the boy went into the bathroom.

A few minutes later the boy came downstairs to join the group assembled in the living room and kitchen. He scanned the rooms and then asked his mother, "Where is Uncle Lou?"

When he was told that he wasn't there, he explained he had just seen him upstairs. The adults looked at the boy; because of his age they hadn't explained to him that his uncle had died one day prior.

There followed constant noises of walking and breathing in the living room late at night — the room Lou had died in.

Around the same time, the owner's brother and his family were saving to buy a house. They were invited to move into the house until they could afford their own. They accepted and moved in.

One evening the parents went out and the older boys had their friends over. The youngest wasn't permitted to come downstairs, as he would get in the way of the older boys' party. He heard noises in the hall and then in the master bedroom. He became frightened so he called down for help. One brother and a few of the braver boys came up to see what was going on. He told them that someone was in their parents' bedroom. They walked to the closed door and heard walking noises on the hardwood flooring beyond the door. They flung the door open and threw on the light. Nothing was there. Then, from behind the closet door, they heard the sound of a wire coat hanger scraping back and forth on the wooden door. They closed in on the closet door and one of them pulled the door open. No one was there; a lone hanger hung on a nail on the door. They searched the room and found nothing; even the window was locked. The youngster was allowed to come down and join the party.

We secured permission to enter and investigate the house. It stood empty, and the owner gave us a key so we could come and go as necessary, to change tapes and so on. The first visit was so Paul and I could conduct a tour and take note of hazards within the house. Part of the front bedroom on the second floor was severely damaged by a water leak. Although the subfloor was still strong, for safety reasons this spot had to be avoided. We were planning to take baseline readings and photos until we heard activity on the upper floor, something moving in the hallway by the stairs. We investigated but found nothing. The second day we introduced a VCR and CCD colour and self-switching infrared camera. The camera was placed on the upper floor, looking down the hall to the front main bedroom and stairwell. As we were about to leave, I set the VCR to record and Paul switched off the hall light. The camera automatically went to infrared mode and I noticed something funny on the monitor, so I asked Paul to come and have a look at it. There seemed to be large white objects swirling around in the hall, nothing we could see with the naked eye. After some debate we couldn't arrive at any firm conclusions, so we simply passed it off as possible dust particles in the air. We left the unit to record and started down the hall to leave when a sound came from a bedroom along the hallway. Paul entered first. As we stepped into the room the floor in the opposite corner made noise, as if someone were moving away from us. We also noticed that this room was close to 10° Fahrenheit colder than the rest of the house, even though all the windows were closed and the furnace was pushing warm air from the floor vents.

The next day, John, Paul, and I arrived to begin the full investigation. We toured the house, starting with the main floor. John had been specifically kept in the dark about the history of the house, as well as the people associated with it. The main floor front room he sensed to be a safe room. Its French doors would have been kept closed. Not many people would have been permitted in this room. We moved on to the living room; he sensed conflict here, arguing, physical violence, dishes flying, injuries, and turmoil. We went upstairs, into the room facing the street; he felt there were secrets hidden here. Secrets about the Second World War and about hiding someone.

John went into the middle room. "There is a lot of energy here, a girl older with a younger mind … undeveloped mind … that of a nine-year-old in an older body. She felt safe in this room … lock the door. She would sit by the window, looking out, rocking in her chair the things she kept; in here was an escape, fantasy. A man close to her (deceased) watched over her. A nice man. There is another man (deceased) who has a lot of conflict with her. Power struggle, arguing, threats, and violence." We moved on to the rear bedroom. He felt it was a storage room; things were hidden there. Disturbed energy. We started downstairs. "The police came here and the military police came here as well. I'm getting many different layers of time," John said.

We headed for the basement; we pulled open the door, and he stepped back. "Something is there: black, crouching, not human, not animal … watching." He stepped forward. "This is an area of strange energy. A place in which time has no meaning." We moved on, but John paused. "It watches, looking down. The basement — things are hidden here. Someone does not want you to find these things that are hidden."

We went for coffee.

Dee, Anita, and Krystal from the Hauntings Research Group arrived and toured the house. I took Dee up to the second floor, and she stopped on the landing. She sensed a man who told her he died from his lungs and heart. He wanted her to know that it was his lungs in particular and due to that complication his heart subsequently failed. She found him to be fairly pleasant. We continued on and toured the upper floor.

We made our way down to the main floor, which was a flurry of activity with the rest of the group taking readings and setting up equipment. We walked into the kitchen, and she paused at the door to the basement. She described a heavy feeling; something was trying to block her. Whatever it was didn't want her gaining any information as to who or what it was. Dee would encounter this entity throughout the night. We continued down to the basement for a look.

Anita investigated the layout of the house. She felt there was something odd about the closet in the upstairs middle room; she couldn't explain it, she just did not like it. She felt it would be a good place to set up a digital recorder to possibly capture electronic voice phenomena (EVP).

They set up cameras on the upper floor: one in the front bedroom looking down the hall and one in the back bedroom looking up the hall. Darrin, an independent film director, arrived at the house.

Paul set up on the main floor, placing one camera at the front door covering the stairs, the hall, and the living room doorway and another in the kitchen doorway looking through the living room to the front door. He also placed a standard tape deck on the landing of the stairs to the upper floor.

Dee and Anita moved to the front room on the main floor to set up in an attempt to communicate with whoever was there. Paul, Krystal, and Darrin followed John into the dining room, where he was going to try to establish communication.

I moved between rooms. All three of them are psychically sensitive and were now going to try to focus that energy through pendulums. John sat down and prepared his pendulum. Anita prepared her pendulum in the other room. They both started asking questions, and I peeked from the front room to the dining room. It was very strange, as they were both asking the same questions at the same time. Both were being blocked by something, and there was no information coming through. I eventually ended up in the dining room beside Paul, with my back to the kitchen. It was at this time that I felt a hand press on my back, between my shoulder blades. I quickly turned and found nothing there.

Anita and Dee came into the living room; they had not received anything and wanted to see what we were getting. John stopped, as he wasn't getting anything either.

We took a short break in the basement.

Dee wanted to try again with the pendulum, so the group assembled in the stairwell to the basement. Dee pulled up a chair at the top of the stairs, next to the door to the kitchen.

"Is there a spirit who wishes to communicate with us?"

Yes.

"Is this the centre of the energy of this house?"

Yes.

"Is this your place?"

Yes.

"Is it okay for us to be here at this time, are we welcome here?"

No.

"Are we welcome here at any time?"

No.

"Is it okay that this place is renovated, altered, changed, walls taken down?"

No.

"Would you like us to leave here?"

Yes.

"Will you allow us to talk with anyone else who is here?"

No.

"Are you holding the others back from speaking to us?"

No.

"Will it be more convenient to come back at another time?"

No.

"Are you specifically holding information from us?"

[No response.]

"Have you hidden something in the walls?"

[Anger.]

"We will be going up into the attic, is that all right?"

No.

"Are you making all the noise, banging around the house?"

Male voice on the EVP: "Yes."

"Are you moving booty? Why don't you tell us where it is?"

We ended the question session here.

We prepared to go to a nearby restaurant to pick up some dinner. Anita decided this was an opportune time to place the digital recorder in the closet of the upstairs middle bedroom. She set the audio recorder and the entire group left the house, locking the front door.

When we returned, Anita retrieved her recorder. When she reviewed it she discovered several odd things. Someone blew into the microphone, but there was no sound of anyone approaching the device; then there was a sound similar to a woman's high-pitched scream. There were sounds of people talking in an echo, their words indistinguishable, then a loud sigh or exhalation followed by a bang and more interference with the microphone. Finally, the recorder picked up our group returning to the house.

We all assembled in the basement to eat our dinner. Everyone stopped talking as we heard banging coming from upstairs, above our heads. Paul and Anita were discussing renovations when the banging came again, then the sound of walking. We grew quiet again and the sounds stopped. They seemed to occur only when there was cover noise. To provoke it, Paul and Anita started talking about renovations again. This brought more noise from the main floor.

After dinner the group split up, heading off into different parts of the house to check equipment, change tapes, and take more readings. Krystal and Dee ended up in the upstairs middle room. They stood quietly for a few minutes. The light in the room started to fade, but within a few moments returned to its original brightness. This happened several times in a row.

We also noticed that throughout the house, especially on the upper floor, cameras with auto-focus had a difficult time focusing and there were things unseen within the depth of field.

The night went on and the investigation came to an end for the group. We had collected some information and confirmed some of what was going on in the house, including the presence of Lou. (I had a great deal of history on the house and people who had lived there, which I did not share with the team. It was amazing that both John and Dee had encountered Lou, who had died of lung cancer in the house. John not only pointed out which room had been the deceased girl's bedroom but was extremely accurate on her disabilities and the use of the main floor parlour with the French doors.) The team packed up and said our good-byes. Paul insisted that we should maintain video surveillance in the house for as long as we could. We set up a wireless camera and a VCR on the main floor, then we all left.

Over the next few weeks, Paul went to the house, changed the tapes, and repositioned the camera to new locations, wherever he thought he'd get the best results. He spent hours reviewing the tapes and was rarely disappointed. There were always sounds of whispers and walking on the audio portion of the tape. When he positioned the camera in the front hall of the main floor, watching the stairs, he recorded a man's voice yelling at the camera, loud and clear, "Get out of this house!" three times in a row.

He eventually set the camera up on the upper floor in the middle bedroom at the rear wall, so it could observe the room's interior and the hallway beyond the door. This yielded strange light phenomena: light that would move up and down the hall, sometimes looking like fog, sometimes bending around the corner and intruding into the room. At times it was so brilliant that it would obliterate all detail of the hallway and floor; at other times it would encroach partially into the room, yet it would not disturb the shadows within the room. Large balls of light would move across the walls and floor, sometimes several of them. Then it happened. Paul called me and said I had to come over right away, we had caught something on tape. I rushed over and we watched. The camera was still in the upper middle bedroom. There were a couple of creaks, then a black shadow the size of a person came out of nowhere and landed directly in the middle of the room, precisely in the centre of the camera field of view. It hit the floor and sped off towards the back of the bedroom to the closet that Anita originally disliked. Then *bang*, another shadow person landed right behind the first and also sped off towards the closet. We tried to view the images in slow motion and frame by frame, but the images disappeared. They seemed to be moving so fast that they were between the frames, only visible at regular speed. This was an incredible catch and we were very pleased.

Our time ran out, and we eventually had to pack up all of our equipment and leave the house.

Good and Evil
Bracebridge

This investigation turned on us, becoming so incredible that it took the team off guard and caused us to question everything: what we knew, what we thought we knew, even our beliefs. Things were occurring that even I didn't want to believe in. It was only after long discussions with those close to me and much soul-searching that I decided, regardless of consequence, that this story should be told here.

It started like most other investigations: a fine family was having difficulty with strange phenomena in their home. Dee and Alison started the initial investigation and were soon joined by Anita, Krystal, and Lloyd. The house was built in the 1840s and backed onto several acres of forest. The house had undergone many changes over its long history and was eventually restored to its former glory. The grounds were well landscaped. However, to the rear of the property there was tall undergrowth at the edge of the forest. Within this undergrowth an old foundation lies hidden. This was thought to be the ruins of an old cannery that once provided jobs for the local people. If one searches the undergrowth, one can still find bottles, jars, and porcelain-coated pans from those days past.

In April 2000 Phil and Ann, wanting to relocate from Northern Ontario, started to look for a suitable home. They viewed many houses, mostly century homes, but it was this house that they had to have. They knew it the first time they walked into it. They had very strong feelings about it, and even though they had looked at bigger homes for less money, this was the one for them. They made their offer and the house became theirs. They were overjoyed. Phil, Ann, and their three daughters, Elizabeth, Aimie, and Emily, moved in right away. Ann was so proud of the beautiful new place that she immediately snapped a quantity of digital photos so she could show her friends what it was like. Ann downloaded the photos on her computer and sent them off to her friends.

A few days later, one of her friends sent her an e-mail regarding the photos. She stated that the house was wonderful but haunted. She explained that she could see three distinct apparitions in the photos: a woman, a little boy, and an old man. Ann was upset but kept the information to herself, hoping that it was all nonsense. Ann re-examined the photos and was somewhat relieved that she couldn't see what her friend had described to her. The first day in the home was quiet, apart from the necessity of unpacking books, dishes, and personal effects.

The next night, that changed. The three girls said goodnight and headed upstairs, taking turns preparing for bed in the bathroom. Elizabeth brushed her teeth and then went to her bedroom. She immediately came rushing down the stairs to the office where her mother was working on the computer, complaining that there was a little boy in her room and he wouldn't leave. Ann made light of the situation and took Elizabeth back upstairs to her room, where they looked for the little boy. She was adamant about what she had seen and told her mother she didn't want to sleep in that room. Ann allowed her to come down to the living room to sleep on the couch while she worked.

Over the next few days, Ann began to experience more subtle phenomena around the house. Lights were turning on and off by themselves, doors were opening and closing, and the catches on the kitchen cabinets were clicking as if someone was deliberately playing with the doors, pulling them open and pushing them shut. One day she smelled a strong scent of quality cherry pipe tobacco in the kitchen. No one in the house smoked. Ann was starting to feel uneasy. She did sense a man in the house and somehow knew that he was a devoted caretaker. He was an older man, and his name started with an H. Two days later Ann smelled the smoke again; she had heard somewhere that if you talk out loud to ghosts, they will sometimes listen to you, so she thought she would give it a try. "Please don't smoke around me!" she said. Ann then noticed that the scent didn't dissipate slowly, but rather disappeared immediately without a trace.

With the ceiling fans now turning on and off by themselves and the sound of heavy furniture being moved around Elizabeth's room, the stress was starting to build in Ann. Occasionally she would find herself standing outside in the driveway, waiting for Phil to arrive home from work.

The following month the situation further escalated, as the family members began hearing their names being called aloud all over the house. Ann and Elizabeth would hear a man whispering their names. Phil was startled by a gravelly man's voice calling his name on the upper floor of the house.

Ann, desperately wanting to find out what was going on in her home, decided to take photos of every room in the house, thinking she would send them off to the friend who had reported seeing spirits in the original photos, hoping for help. As she downloaded the photos onto her computer she realized that she did not need to send them off to her friend, as she could now see the spirits for herself. Ann was frightened of what was in her home and the fact that she could now see them. She went back and opened the original photos, and even though she had enlarged them and examined them closely the first time and saw nothing, she could see them now. The images were quite clear and just as they had been described to her.

Phil and Emily were not reporting seeing anything unusual in the house; however, Ann and Elizabeth started to see things on a regular basis, including faint shapes of people moving around the house. Aimie saw them too, although not as often. One day Elizabeth awoke to see a very solid-looking young girl in her bedroom, smiling at her; she was wearing a pink dress with white bloomers showing beneath. Her hair was shoulder length, curly blond. She told her mother right away about the incident, and what Elizabeth described was exactly what Ann had captured in one of her photos. On another occasion the girl was seen wearing a dark hooded cloak. No one could pick up on a name for the little girl, but both Ann and Elizabeth somehow felt the female spirit's name was Mary.

Throughout the first summer in their new home Ann's health began to deteriorate rapidly. She found that she could hardly walk at times and became bedridden, often using hot packs and painkillers. Ann had always been in good health and could not understand what was happening. She consulted her doctors, and they were at a loss to discover any medical reason for her decline. Ann was becoming so nervous about being in the house that when she was alone she turned on all the lights and played the stereo. This didn't help, as she could still hear the whispers and a female who liked to sing upstairs, and she could still feel the roving cold spots and, most terrifying of all, the direct touches from someone unseen. Most of the time when the children left for school Ann would also leave, spending hours wandering the mall or visiting anyone she could spend time with. She was trying desperately to avoid staying in the house that she had fallen in love with not so long ago.

By October of that year Ann was nearing the end of her rope. The stress of the phenomena occurring in and around the house, the deterioration of her health, and the deep concern for her family were taking their toll. She talked the situation over with Phil, and they decided that she would ask the priest from the local church for help. Ann spoke to the priest and he agreed to come by the house.

The day he was scheduled to come by Ann rushed around picking up after the kids and kept busy tidying the place. She fluffed the pillows on the sofa and put things where they belonged. She stopped and looked around: everything was neat and tidy. She was somewhat nervous about the visit, as she didn't know quite what to expect. She tried to kill time with small tasks in anticipation of his arrival. It was then that she somehow felt Mary was close by; she decided to tell her what was about to happen. Ann said out loud, "Mary, a priest is coming by to bless the house. This is to bring peace to the home and not to send you, the boy, or the man away." Ann waited a few moments, feeling a little silly about talking out loud by herself. But then she continued, "I hope you are really here and that you heard me explain this." A couple of seconds later Ann caught a movement out of the corner of her eye and turned to see a penny fall from the ceiling to the sofa, landing with a plop on the cushion. Ann walked over, picked it up, and looked at it. It was a 1978 Canadian penny; she just looked at it and wondered if the date had any significance. "Thank you!" Ann said aloud.

The priest arrived and they talked for a few minutes, then the priest blessed each room in the house. Ann was surprised that the house felt different right away; she knew the spirits were still there, but whatever was causing her all the fear and unease was now gone. She walked the priest out onto the front walkway and thanked him for his help.

In the late fall the family set aside a day to go out back and do yard work, cleaning up and raking leaves to prepare for the coming snow. It was a lovely day and they worked and played. As the sun started to sink on the horizon, they noticed lights inside the house turning on and off. Phil and

Ann investigated, and no one was found to be in the house. They did find that several lights that were previously off had been turned on. Soon after, at 7:30 p.m., the television set in the sitting room came on by itself. Both Phil and Ann examined the television to make sure there wasn't a time set for it to come on automatically. It continued, so they unplugged the TV. Hoping that might have fixed the problem, they plugged it in again. Nothing seemed to help, and this continued for two more weeks. Finally, they unplugged the set and left it unplugged. The night after they unplugged it, the TV turned on again, having been plugged in somehow. At the same time, the stereo in the living room turned on by itself. This happened for a couple of nights, and then stopped altogether.

Dee and Alison met Ann at a restaurant in Port Perry; they started talking about ghosts, and Ann invited them to her house whenever they could make it out to Bracebridge. Dee was intrigued by what she had been told and decided to go out and have a look for herself. Dee made arrangements with Ann to visit her and see the house.

When Dee arrived they went into the kitchen to talk. Ann made coffee. While Dee was sitting at the table she felt something tugging at the back of her shirt and immediately sensed that it was the little boy. The unseen boy was persistent and continued to pull at Dee's shirt while they had coffee and talked. After coffee they decided to tour the house. They stopped at Elizabeth's room and went in. Ann felt that the little boy, who, according to Elizabeth, was named Timothy or Timmy, had died in this room from pneumonia. Dee agreed that he had died in this room, which was his room at one time, but it was kidney failure and not pneumonia. Dee then sensed another presence, that of a woman who came close and stood next to Dee. Ann stated that her name was Mary. They walked through the house, Mary staying close by. They came back down to the main floor, and Dee looked out the back patio door towards the yard. Her gaze was drawn towards the forest. Dee studied it intently for a few minutes, then turned to Ann. "There is something in the woods that I just don't like!"

Ann told her, "Elizabeth doesn't like it either, she will no longer go out to the backyard by herself."

Dee told Ann that she would like to conduct an investigation of the property to further explore what was going on. Ann agreed.

Ann frequently saw someone walking past open doors in the home, even when no one else was home. The lights kept turning on and off and doors opened and closed by themselves. One night Phil and Ann were awakened by the bed shaking, slowly and deliberately; each blamed the other. But when they got up and out of the bed that they noticed that it was still moving. Nothing else in the room was shaking. Elizabeth was starting to complain of hearing someone on the stairs late at night. Then one night Ann woke to see a woman and a young boy standing at the bottom of her bed, watching her. They quickly dissipated; the whole thing was unnerving.

Anita and Dee came back for a preliminary investigation to see what further information they could pick up on. They toured the house, finding that the most comforting place was the front porch. They decided that this would be the place to come during any investigations that might follow for team meetings and discussions while on the property.

As they toured the home they started to pick up on an old man who smoked a pipe. They both concentrated on trying to discover his name. It came to them and they spoke it out loud at exactly the same time: "Harlan!" He communicated with them and tried to grasp some of the modern ideas and technology; he also communicated about what he was familiar with, back in his time.

After some time they moved to the back of the house and yard. They looked at each other as they were both sensing an African-American male who seemed malicious near the edge of the woods. He seemed to be attached to the girls of Ann's family. He would just stand there and watch. Anita and Dee compared notes later and felt that this person was responsible for the death of a young girl, who would have been approximately age nine at the time. Ann mentioned that Elizabeth had seen the apparition of a young girl in the house some time ago.

Later that day they went down to the woods. Anita stated that she sensed him there and started calling him out, daring him to do something. She sensed his name to be Jacob. Dee started to take random digital photos of the forest. It wasn't until later that night, when Dee downloaded her photos onto her computer, that she noticed within the trees and brush an African-American man, naked from the waist up, standing there, his shape merging with the flora, making him appear stealthy.

A few days after they had conducted their preliminary investigation of the house Emily spotted a black shadow of what looked like a large person on the back porch, right at the patio door. Emily had never experienced anything like that before, and it scared her. Later in the week the girls had a pool party and invited several of their friends over. Some of the girls became nervous after seeing a man standing at the back fence, watching them. It was after this incident that Ann became extremely concerned, as the children were now refusing to go anywhere near the yard.

Lloyd would stop by to see Ann and work on researching the history of the house. One day he stopped in and they went into the kitchen to look over some old files. Ann said she would make some coffee. She got up and went to the kitchen counter to set up the coffee maker, but was startled to discover it was already on. Ann checked it and found it must have just been turned on as the water was only slightly warm.

Ann called Dee and told her of the new sightings and developments. Dee told her they would come back to the house right away.

Anita and Dee returned to the house and decided that they needed to place a ward over the backyard. Dee performed a Native American ceremony and Anita performed a Wiccan ceremony at the same time. This would keep anything negative out of the yard and away from the house. In the weeks to come, Ann was amazed that the children had lost their fear of going into the yard. They would willingly go swimming without needing Phil or Ann to watch over them. It seemed that the problem was solved.

Dee contacted me, telling me about the events at Ann's house and that they planned to go out on the weekend to continue their investigation; they wanted to know if I would like to join them. I jumped at the opportunity and started preparing my equipment as soon as I hung up the phone.

Lloyd stopped in to see Ann in order to discuss some of the history of the house that he had discovered at the local library. He brought his five-year-old daughter along. They sat at the kitchen table for some time, talking, and his daughter became bored. She stood up and went to the living room, but stopped at the patio door. "There's a little girl!" she said aloud.

Ann and Lloyd went to see what she was talking about and noticed that she was visibly upset.

"What little girl?" her father asked.

"That little girl in the forest, she got all wet and her bones floated to the top!" she replied, her little finger pointing.

Ann and Lloyd looked from her to the woods; they saw nothing out there.

Dee, Anita, Krystal, Lloyd, Alison, and I arrived at the house that weekend and met with Ann. We assembled on the front porch and discussed the events and our plans for that evening. Anita sensed right away that Harlan was there.

It was time to prepare for the evening; the team split up, heading off to retrieve their individual equipment. A few minutes later the team reconvened in the backyard of the house. Anita said this was where the spirit named Jacob would come. We wanted to collect base-line readings of the area before it started to get dark. We entered the forest through a small opening, which led to a path. Anita, Dee, Krystal, Lloyd, and I moved in as the path widened. Dee started her tape recorder. Krystal was filming and Anita was taking digital photos. Lloyd and I set up a criss-cross pattern, recording electromagnetic field readings on the gauss meter. Nothing out of the ordinary was found in the EMF.

Lloyd and Krystal found what appeared to be the remains of a very old still; Dee felt that there might be an interesting story about Prohibition in Ontario to be discovered here as well.

After everyone was satisfied with the collection of data, we started back towards the yard. As the group headed down the path, Dee's tape recorder picked up a little girl's voice calling for someone, followed by a scream. Upon review of the tape we could not be sure if these sounds were in fact phenomena to do with something that had taken place in the woods or if they were natural sounds of kids, possibly playing on the next property.

As we entered the yard the group broke up, some making notes, others taking even more photos. Dee took my compass, wanting to get a bearing. The compass refused to settle and the needle kept spinning. She finally laid it on the ground, thinking that she could have something on her that was making it react the way it was. As she watched it she moved to varying distances, starting at about a foot away, eventually moving to three feet from it. This had no effect on the sporadic motion of compass's needle. She began taking several photos of the compass as I walked up to her. I watched it for a moment, then checked the area with my gauss meter. I did find an anomalous reading of 2.5 milligauss in a one-foot-wide by two-foot-high area around the compass. Eventually the compass needle did settle on a point. The area was scanned again with the gauss meter and the EMF was now zero.

An old stone foundation behind the house, hidden in the forest undergrowth, piqued our curiosity. This was possibly an old cannery that was reported to have been on the property or an older house that was rumoured to have burned down. Lloyd, being a skilled mason by trade, decided to wade in to investigate the structure's remains. He fought off the dense mosquitoes as he worked, soon emerging with his findings. He reported that the high quality of the workmanship indicated that this was an important structure, like a home, not a secondary structure like a barn or other outbuilding. He had an idea and went to get a hammer from the shed. He returned a few minutes later with his hammer, a Frisbee, and regular white vinegar. Again he waded into the brush going to the old foundation; he used the hammer to break off a few small pieces of stone. He came back and crumbled these into the upside down Frisbee. He explained that if the vinegar interacted with the limestone and produced a fizz, it would indicate a time span of more than two hundred years, give or take a few years. He poured in the vinegar and there was a definite fizz. He said there were more complicated tests we could do, but we didn't have the equipment to perform them at this time. It was at that point I realized that Lloyd may have been influenced by the old *MacGyver* TV series as a child — but then, weren't we all!

We finished our notes and headed to the house, where we had a meal and convened on the front porch to go over our notes and theories and plan out what we needed to do next.

At just after 10:00 p.m. the group re-entered the forest. As we proceeded, constant flashes from the team's digital cameras pushed away
the darkness. Lloyd and I once again scanned the area with the gauss
meter; we came across one particular tree that produced varied gauss
readings from 1 to 3 milligauss. This same tree had been tested earlier in the day, producing no unusual results. This tree attracted me
because it had old wooden planks nailed to it, as if at one time they
had been used as a ladder to climb the tree, possibly to access a tree
fort. Any further evidence of a tree fort was now gone.

We started to walk out of the woods when Anita's flashlight failed,
although the batteries were brand new; later she tried a new bulb, which
also failed. We reached the clearing and chose a spot about sixty feet from
the forest to use as a base. We brought some chairs and our equipment
down from the house and set up.

Dee stepped forward and asked Lloyd to take her hand and ground
her, as she was going to attempt to channel whatever was out in those
woods; she felt something was there. She opened herself up and immediately felt a man standing behind some brush, watching, waiting to see what
she was going to do. Dee requested his name, but he refused to say. She
asked again, and Lloyd was openly startled as he heard a reply: "Jacob."

The male presence in the woods moved forward towards the clearing
and started pushing his energy at Dee. Dee told him not to push her and
to keep his distance. Dee broke contact at that point.

Lloyd stated that he felt there was something wrong with the
entity's leg.

Dee said, "The right leg," and he immediately agreed.

Dee sensed the entity again and felt he was telling us that these were
his woods and that we didn't belong there. Dee made it clear to him that
they were not his woods. He began pushing at her again.

We moved the chairs into a circle and sat down. Lloyd offered to
ground Dee once again.

In a few moments she re-established contact with the entity, then
asked Lloyd what he sensed. He said, "A large piece of wood flying
through the air."

Dee was getting a different image, one of the entity rushing the
clearing. He could not enter the clearing and became angry. He was

trying to intimidate us into leaving. He began calling other entities, which came to support him, congregating behind him. Lloyd saw them as well and stated, "He's like a foreman, he's like, ah, ah, I don't know what you would call it, a lead hand or something. He's telling these guys what to do, right! Am I right?"

Lloyd wasn't aware that on a previous visit Dee and Anita had sensed this entity and spoke to the homeowner, telling her that this person was at one time a lead hand and henchman for a powerful businessman who lived in town and whom nobody crossed.

The team stood their ground; everyone saw the black shadows moving on the edge of the forest, trying to advance.

The entity could not cross into the opening, and it was Dee's feeling that he was going to use the others to cross the barrier for him. Anita, for safety's sake, walked out to the edge of the forest and created a ward to stop them from crossing into the clearing. As she did so, several photos were taken of her in rapid succession. The first two simply showed her walking along the edge of the forest, the third showed hundreds of red spots surrounding her, and the fourth showed the spots dissipating. The entities spread out along the perimeter of the clearing, looking for a way to enter. Lloyd reported seeing a very large entity, which Dee confirmed. Krystal was concerned about the others being able to charge us. Neither Dee nor Anita was sure, but Dee offered, "If they haven't done so by now, then most likely they can't." Even I found very little comfort in that.

They finally decided to retreat, but instead of turning away from us, they literally walked backwards and faded off into the woods.

Anita was receiving information; she was becoming very frustrated.

"He's behind someone … he's behind someone. There's someone else. The black man is standing towards … the right side, right where the weeds are tall, but not the trees. There are two of them. The black man is standing behind the white man. Come on … He's standing behind, like, look what I can do! Why is he behind him? … He has a smug look on his face. I can't see who's in front of him. Standing just behind not beside. He's all smug and he's all big. He knows something that we don't. He looks like he's untouchable."

Lloyd jumped in, "Oh it's Lyrch, he's the tall guy. Is he really tall?"

"I can't get who he's standing behind. He's in shadow. The black man is standing here, but behind the line. There's a man, not as big, small, slight." She stopped, unable to get the image.

I noticed a black shadow move up near the back of the house, then quickly disappear.

When Dee reviewed her tape she found an anomalous ticking noise on it. This noise is sometimes recorded in close proximity to spirit activity.

I unpacked the parabolic microphone and handed it to Anita, whereupon the batteries failed. Trying to lighten the mood, I told her that she was too hard on batteries and couldn't touch the equipment anymore.

I changed the batteries and handed the microphone to Krystal, who moved to the edge of the woods facing the path and listened. She heard what sounded like a woman whispering.

Dee asked Lloyd what his impressions were while he was acting as a ground. He said, "Guys, a group of men. I would say there were six or seven of them. One tall guy. The thing that stands out the most to me is a piece of wood flying through the air, whatever that may mean, and the pain in my leg, which coincided with the pain you felt in your leg. And the name Jacob."

Krystal listened intently for a few more minutes, then heard, "Ummm, you smell sweet!" and some whispering. She was not sure if the voice was a man or a woman.

I took the microphone and listened; after a minute I heard voices, although I could not make out what they were saying. Then movement. I passed the device off to Dee, and she heard a male voice enticing her, calling, "Come, come in and see me!"

We finally broke and went back to the house for a break. We had some tea and discussed what had happened. Lloyd reported seeing a black shadow moving around the rear of the house. Elizabeth also reported seeing human forms in the yard and on the deck. Alison took some pictures and used the owner's computer to download the photos. After she played with the contrast, the images verified what Elizabeth reported seeing.

Lloyd showed us his hand, which was swollen and extremely hot; he complained that it tingled as well. It was the hand he had used to hold Dee's hand while he was grounding her. Dee told him to hold his hand out and placed one of her hands under and the other hand over his for a few moments. We watched as the swelling went down, the heat dissipating quickly. After a few minutes he said his hand felt much better.

Time ran out and we had to pack up the equipment for the drive home. We planned our next visit, then said our goodbyes.

It was early in the day a week later, and Lloyd decided to drop in and see how Ann was doing and follow up on some research. They met and had coffee, talking for a while about what was going on in and around the house. Through their research, they had discovered that there was once a distillery at the back of Ann's property, deep within the forest, run by a wealthy, powerful man within the community. A few of his employees at one time lived in cabins on the property. These cabins had been torn down in the 1940s.

Lloyd excused himself and went off to use the main floor washroom. When he was coming back out of the washroom he felt something strange. The room was extremely cold, and he felt an electrical tingle. He turned and looked towards the dining room, but froze as his eyes fell upon a man. Goosebumps rose on his arms and the hair on the back of his neck stood on end. The man was short between, 5'1" and 5'3", with a balding head with curly grey hair. His face was chubby; he was wearing an old greyish blue coat that was short in the front and stopped at his waist but was long in the back and went down to almost the back of his knees. He was leaning on the dining room table, hands open, palms down, looking into the front room. Lloyd could not see what he was looking at. The man was either not aware of Lloyd or more focused on something else. Lloyd wasn't sure what to do; he finally called out to Ann to bring her camera. She wasn't sure what he had said, so Lloyd turned and yelled, "Bring your camera!" But when he turned back, the image was gone. Ann came rushing in and noticed right away that the room was freezing. Lloyd showed her the goosebumps on his arms and told her what he had seen. They walked around the rooms a few times, then went outside to warm up.

Fear is when you find yourself in a situation where you are unsure of what may occur next. All your senses become heightened, fueled by adrenaline. But as scared as you may be, you know you can always leave.

Terror is when you are pushed beyond the edge of fear by circumstances beyond your control. Your senses fail; the only thing that you are aware of is the sound of blood pumping in your ears, and you realize that whatever is scaring you is in control. Escape is no longer an option, as you now know your fate is in its hands.

The first indication that this was not simply a typical haunting but rather something much more daunting was the discovery of what Harlan truly was. No one on the team was prepared for what was to occur next.

If one believes in evil things that permeate this world as well as the next, then it is only natural to believe that the opposite must also exist. While in communication with him, Dee and Anita attempted to gain some insight into Harlan and his intentions. He appeared, as he normally had been seen in the house, as a frail little old man who wore work clothes. But it was at this moment, during this particular communication, that this false apparition shifted, burning away like fog to reveal his true self. Light, powerful yet peaceful, emanated from within him, but also from without, encompassing him and acting as a guardian. Then he was gone, and only the familiar pipe smoke remained in the air.

When I learned of this, it excited me and at the same time caused me great concern. It was a personal revelation to know of such a being, and it restored faith in my personal beliefs. The concern came almost immediately afterwards, as I felt something like Harlan would not be sent as a protector against mere ghostly entities. For me, fear stepped forward; for the sake of the investigation and the family living on this property, I had to push those feelings aside. It was a personal choice to stay, and this is where that difference would eventually surface — the difference between fear and terror — I just didn't know it yet. On that day, as we arrived to continue our investigation, we discovered that Harlan was nowhere to be found.

Anita sat on the front porch, as she normally did, the porch being the safe place. After a few minutes she looked up and stated that something was very wrong: the house was very different, and Harlan was not present. Dee looked at her and, unable to sense him, acknowledged the fact that he was indeed missing. Anita looked away, stating that she was beginning to get a severe headache.

We all had our own feelings about what that meant and how the house seemed, but we were here to do a job and nobody talked about it, not yet anyways. Everyone started to get up and wander into the house, trying to get a better feeling on what had happened, where he had gone. Some of us bypassed the house and headed directly into the yard to take some baseline readings.

The place felt different. I couldn't pinpoint what it was; I just knew in my gut that I didn't like the feeling. Shadows skulked around, watching when you least expected it.

It started in the basement. I had moved some equipment down to the bottom of the stairs, with Elizabeth and Aimie helping me retrieve cables and place microphones. I was about to connect the video surveillance camera to the monitor as Elizabeth was heading up the stairs to fetch an extension cord from the kitchen. That's when I noticed something grab her leg on the stairs. I couldn't see who or what was grabbing her, so I moved in closer, thinking she was going to fall backwards. She kicked and pulled, and I called out to her. She broke free and ran up the stairs, through the door, and into the kitchen, swinging the door closed behind her. As I watched, this *something*, still invisible to me, hit the kitchen door hard and pushed it open, slamming into the wall. I headed up the stairs; the loud crash had brought the rest of the team to the kitchen. It was interesting to note later, when the audiotapes were reviewed, that during the incident, just after I called out to her by name, another man's voice said her name aloud. At the time of the recording, I was the only male not only in the basement, but also in the entire house.

Dee, Anita, Krystal, Aimie, and I went to the basement. We were going to try to make contact with the young female entity that had been seen so often in and around the house. Dee, Anita, and Krystal moved deeper into the basement. Aimie and I stayed near the stairs, watching them. I felt my shoulders hunch and the hair on my arms rise, as if a low-voltage electrical field was against my back; I recognized this feeling. I turned to look at Aimie, and at the same time we whispered to each other, "It's here." Anita looked over at us and Aimie told her something was there with us. Anita looked past us and said there was nothing there, then she looked at me, and the expression on my face told her otherwise. I just nodded my head yes. This evil thing was telling Aimie that he had a knife and was going to plunge it into her back. I turned to try and face it, a difficult task when you can't see your adversary. Aimie moved towards Anita and stood in front of her, and Anita consoled her by putting her hands on her shoulders. The thing lingered a moment longer, then it was gone. But it continued to move among us, blocking Dee and Anita's ability to detect it. For some reason the girls and I could feel when it came close to us. When I mentioned it was in the room, Dee and Anita would hone in on it. I soon realized what it was doing. It was going from group to group and listening, collecting intelligence. Soon it was causing us to act and react, testing us. This thing, whatever it was, was smart.

We set up a dual CCD colour infrared camera, monitor, and VCR, pointing out from the yard towards the forest. The fog was thick — on the monitor it looked like a major snowstorm. The infrared was picking up the water molecules within the fog and we could watch them move and swirl around. Not exactly what we wanted to see, but we left it running anyways.

Krystal, Anita, and I were talking about the events when Anita looked over and saw something on the monitor. The three of us looked at the fog; she wanted to be sure, so instead of saying what she saw she waited to see if we could pick up the image. It was faint at first, then became more defined. The image appeared to be an old claw foot bathtub or something of that shape. But how could we be getting something like this on the monitor? It didn't make any sense at all. We called the others out to see it. As they arrived, the fog swirled and the image changed to what now appeared to be a double set of heavy doors. This remained for a few moments, but each time the fog swirled the image would alternate between the tub thing and the doors. Dee asked if the machine was recording. I said yes. Alison took some digital photos of the monitor screen. None of us could make sense of what we were seeing. Anita and I, grasping at straws, thought we were being shown something from within the house. Anita, Krystal, and I headed into the house to see if there were any similarities between the images and the structural features of the home.

We stopped at the top of the upper floor stairs. Everything there seemed close to what we were looking for, but it was all wrong. This wasn't the image we had seen on the monitor. Krystal suggested we go downstairs to the living room to discuss the situation. We agreed and headed down into the living room. Anita was obviously agitated and was nervously rubbing and pulling at her hair.

"What's going on?" Krystal asked.

"Whatever it is, it's playing games with us!" Anita answered.

Then I had that feeling again, as if I had just backed into an electrical field. I leaned over and whispered to Anita, "It's here!"

Anita grabbed her chest. "The air is thick, it's getting too big!"

I felt it move and followed the feeling to a spot between the chair and the couch. "Here!"

Anita moved to my position and shook her head no.

"It's gone!" I said.

"I can feel him, he was just standing right here, but now he's ..." Anita said.

"He's just here, there and everywhere!" Krystal said.

"Yeah, he's friggin' cocky!" Anita said.

We headed back outside to the surveillance equipment.

We watched the images come and go on the monitor. The image that had looked like an bathtub was starting to resemble a table with a high curved edge on it, something you would find at a morgue. There was definitely someone on it, and the image of several people started to appear, standing around all in black. We just couldn't understand what we were looking at and how it related to the property.

Every time some of the team broke away from the main group, the unseen force would move in to either frighten or eavesdrop; eventually we could not function, as we seemed to be always yelling at it or telling it where to go.

We went into the house for a break and to review the tape. The tape did not capture any of the images that we had seen, but at least Alison had a good image on her camera. It was late and we decided to call an end to the investigation for the time being.

It was a short time after the end of our investigation at Ann's house that some of the teenaged relatives of various group members showed a great deal of interest in what we do as paranormal investigators. We didn't want to discourage them by saying no to an outing, so we decided to take the interested ones out to a location that was reputed to be haunted but had been proven not to be by the Hauntings Research Group. It had all the necessary ambiance required for the young group to learn, but was totally benign. About fourteen of us ended up on "Ghost Road," an old country road surrounded by forest that encroached to the very edge of the road. The teens were given digital cameras, electromagnetic field detectors, and parabolic microphones to experiment with. They were having a great time.

I wandered away from the group and was near the end of the line of vehicles parked on the side of the road. I was walking near a van belonging to the group when I heard a shuffling sound on the gravel, near the rear of the van. I thought it was an animal, so I went to investigate. As I moved close, it hit me: I could sense this thing, and it was very powerful. I stepped back and called Anita over. Anita walked over to me and there was some banging in or around the van. My skin tingled and goosebumps rose on my arms. It took her a few seconds to pick up on it, and then she looked at me. "It's in the van … the driver's seat," she stated.

"Let's have a look," I said as I began moving closer to the van.

She stood her ground. "I'd rather not."

I walked up to the driver's window, which was down, and shone my flashlight in. Nothing. I looked in and scanned the interior and still found nothing. The feeling was gone.

What was strange about this incident was what I knew: first, that it was the entity from Ann's house; and second, that when I went to go check the van, I felt completely safe because somehow I knew this entity didn't want a confrontation. What I didn't know was why it was out there with us. The fact that it was disturbed me.

Not long afterwards the expedition finished and we packed up and said our goodbyes. Dee discovered that her car had somehow become locked, but didn't really pay any attention to it. Some of the group headed off to the coffee shop for a drink and to talk about future plans. Dee and I went in her car; Anita and Krystal went together. We bought our coffee and stood in the parking area, talking. Again Dee's car somehow became locked; this time her keys were inside the car. She had to call her husband, Gary, at home, wake him up, and ask him to drive out with the extra set of keys, which he did.

It was now really late and we all headed home. Dee drove me to my place and dropped me off, we said goodnight, and she left. As she drove home, it came over her like a blast of negative feelings that something was in the back seat of her car, watching her. It was so powerful that she had the urge to pull over and get out, but she came to a point where it started to anger her as much as it scared her, and her attitude changed. She told it that she wasn't about to react to its crap and that it wasn't welcome and should leave. Soon after, the negative feelings dissipated and she was fine the rest of the way home.

The following day Anita's father and her stepmother, Judy, came over to help her do some work around her home. Everyone was outside working on planter boxes when Judy went into the house to use the bathroom; she was the only one in the house at the time. As she was heading back outside she discovered that the front door was locked. This was a dead bolt–type lock that had to be physically turned to engage the bolt. She opened the door, went outside, and asked Anita if she had locked the door. Anita hadn't, and besides, to lock the door from outside would require the key. No one had been near the porch or door. Later in the day Dee arrived at Anita's house and went inside. As she was standing in the foyer, Dee sensed something near her. She told Anita. Just as Anita stated that she didn't sense anything, the feeling came over her. Its energy was quite strong, though neither of them felt that it was malicious.

Later that night, after everyone had left, Anita settled in to watch a movie in the living room. The heavy curtains behind her were drawn closed. All of a sudden, the curtains flew open. Both sides flew across their tracks in opposite directions. She jumped from the couch and looked at them. She couldn't sense what was there with her, and that frightened her. She rushed to the phone and called Dee, asking her to come over right away. Dee agreed, so Anita went to the front door and unlocked it, then went into the kitchen to make tea.

Dee arrived at the door and found it locked. Anita was in the kitchen when she felt something standing over her. She could feel the breath on the back of her neck and on her ear. Dee pounded on the door, and Anita yelled for her to come in, thinking that it was unlocked, as she had left it. After a few moments, Anita came out of the kitchen and opened the door. Dee entered and they went into the dining room, where it was now the strongest. She demanded that it leave and stated that it didn't belong there and that it was not welcome. Dee called for spiritual assistance to force whatever this thing was out of the house. They sat there for about an hour and a half and nothing more happened.

Dee mentioned that previously there had been a dark entity watching her from her basement window.

The investigation continues.

Photos of the rear door of a dwelling taken at night. Note: the cut-out, enlarged sections of the photos show an image at the door.

This is the entrance to the tunnel where ghosts dressed in Civil War uniforms have been sighted, even though this tunnel was added in 1965.

Photo of an empty building. Note the image of a face in the bottom left-hand pane (enlarged in the cut-out).

Another photo of a different building in the same area. Note the image of a woman's head in the right window (image enlarged in cut-out).

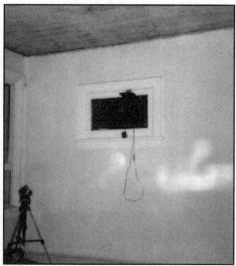

Two photos of the same room. The first is a control photo. The second shows strange light patterns on the wall.

The outside of a vacant building. Note in the cut-out the image of a woman sitting in one of the windows.

Theories

The most important fundamental laws and facts of physical science have all been discovered, and these are now so firmly established that the possibility of them ever being supplemented in consequence of new discoveries is exceedingly rare.

— A.A. Michelson (1852–1931)

I cannot help fearing that men may reach a point where they look on every new theory as a danger, every innovation as a toilsome trouble, every social advance as a first step toward revolution, and that they may absolutely refuse to move at all.

— Alexis de Tocqueville (1803–1882)

Man will occasionally stumble over the truth, but usually manages to pick himself up, walk over or around it, and carry on.

— Winston S. Churchill (1874–1965)

The observations and theories in this book are put forth with the hope that other paranormal investigators will help prove or disprove the information provided. It will be through many of the undiscovered bright minds out there that solid, verifiable solutions will be assembled, pushing our study into the scientific mainstream and bringing forth advancements in parapsychology. As we forge into unknown territory on our quest for knowledge I am sure that errors will be made from time to time. This normally opens the door to criticism, which in turn allows discussion. I believe that it will be in these future discussions that we will arrive at the truth about life after death.

Over the years I have seen many unexplained phenomena — some for various reasons, most because I went looking for them.

Someone told me, "Once you see these things they become much more easily seen." Looking back I have to believe that this statement is true: the telltale signs are readily recognizable to those who already have a mental template of what they are looking for. However, as an investigator, one cannot take anything for granted. I have reluctantly placed to the side many really intriguing events that suggest the existence of life after death simply because they didn't fit my criteria. As investigators we have a responsibility to represent what we find as truthfully and as accurately as we can. I use a method that relies on corroboration from several sources on the same subject; if any one source fails then the information is set aside and we move on. This method uses every resource available to verify a single piece of information. For example, if I were to use psychics, I would use only people who are legitimate and trustworthy. Even then, you are at the mercy of their testimony and interpretation of the information, so it is best to use at the minimum two psychics under controlled measures (meaning they work independently and have no communication with each other). This way information gained by each can be examined and compared to see if there is corroboration of facts, such as names, dates, and events. I also like to use a full range of equipment while the psychics are at work, from video surveillance to tape recorders to environmental sensors. When you add up all the collected data you get a sense of what the truth may be. It is in those rare moments when you have confirmation of hard facts — like names, dates, and events — between independent psychics that it becomes interesting. Couple this with information obtained by EVP detailing the same information and other equipment that indicates what is perceived as ghostly activity and you may actually have something. It doesn't stop there, however — the information only becomes valuable if you can confirm the details received through records, archives, or people who know about the history you are investigating. Once this is achieved then you have evidence that some form of communication has occurred — what type, of course, is another matter.

In my early years I read all that I could on the subject of ghosts and hauntings. I looked up to the leaders in parapsychology, following their theories with great enthusiasm. It wasn't until many years later, when I started conducting field investigations and experiments, that I ran into trouble. I wanted to learn how they manifested, where they existed, and, most importantly, what combined elements formed what we perceived as an apparition. The trouble came as I tried to fit old theory into what my observations and data were telling me. There seemed to be some great conflict. When I compared the theory to the observation, logic was nowhere to be found; this became a perplexing conundrum. Was there no room for logic within parapsychology? Why? How could I continue my work, how could I apply any type of scientific method without its basis in logic? How could this happen? It took me more than a year to finally come to the conclusion that I had been led astray. I was discovering that most of these theories were wrong, or simply misguided. I found this somewhat disheartening and yet at the same time quite exciting. It was a long road of discovery to understand why those before us would have led us in the directions that they did. These were trusted people within society, pillars of the community who were being called upon to answer impossible questions by the general public at a moment's notice. We have to understand that most were practitioners within the local church and had a predisposed ideology of what was occurring prior to even looking into the occurrences. In order to maintain their standing they had very little choice but to provide some reasonable explanation as to what they thought was taking place. Imagine for a moment that there was a cry for help going out to some of the most revered people within the community and the response was "We just don't know." They had to provide an answer. Those answers became the beginning of the modern spiritual movement, and theories were built upon them. What came next were those who felt they could earn a living working in the field of parapsychology, turning out book after book on the subject using the old theories without any proof whatsoever. This caused great harm, as the scientific community turned its back on the entire subject. For those who wanted to do work in parapsychology there seemed to be but one starting point: the old theories. From them we compiled what looked like new theories, but which were only extensions of the old ones, distorted and twisted to fit like a square peg into a round hole. This just added to the confusion and deepened the mystery. This was conformity at its best — it helped sell books, and one never had to step out on a ledge or chance ridicule from other paranormal investigators. Most sit on the fence and silently wait for some trend to appear, then they promote this idea as if it were their own. If you follow some of the bigger websites you will see this quite clearly. As the trend subsides and something new comes into view they change directions, and the old idea is attacked as if they knew it just didn't make any sense. In any event, it doesn't take much to see the ridiculous state of affairs we are left in. Instead of following trends, one must step back, examine the sum of past information, apply some logic, and come to one's own conclusions. The best example of the confusion we are faced with is what we call spirit energy. Entities, ghosts, spooks, specters, shades, apparitions, spirits, shadows — the list goes on and on. Even the term *poltergeist* has its own distinction. Each name carries with it its own attributes. Logically, if what we are studying are the souls of those departed, and every person acts and reacts differently, then how can we assign names that distinguish the spirits by their actions? The list is either much too long or much too short. I always maintain people are people, dead or alive, and they will act and react as they are accustomed.

Theories

So what makes a ghost a ghost? If we examine the historical reports in parapsychology and believe that life continues after death, then the philosophical explanation is that a ghost is a living person removed from the physical, but still retaining all their mental attributes. But ask the same question scientifically and it becomes difficult and complex. There are many equally important elements that must exist and come together to create such an entity. There is no black and white, no clearly defined lines, just as there are none should one ask what makes a living person a person. We could go to the library and scan thousands of volumes of medical texts regarding information on what we are and how we work, but there are just as many questions as there are answers about what we are. How does the human mind work? What is reality? To science, consciousness is an anomaly that cannot be explained. If we look at a person in front of us, light waves reflect off their body; this reflection is focused onto the cells in the retina of our eye, causing a chemical reaction that releases a flow of electrons. Neurons then send electrical impulses to the brain's visual cortex. There this information is interpreted, and we see the image of the person is in our conscious mind. The reality of the world is perceived by our senses — touch, sight, sound, taste, and smell — and filtered through our mind. People and objects are no more than clouds of atoms and sub-atomic particles. We may recognize objects due to their particular harmonic frequency, but look at the same objects through infrared or ultraviolet (UV) imaging and the world changes; in a sense, our perception of reality also changes.

Dreams are in essence another reality. When we dream we are capable of using all the senses and experiencing sensations such as pleasure or pain. The mind can create all of the emotions without the physical body. Even though we are examining something that has been studied for generations, the question of life after death and ghosts seems to mystify us. Having said that, I believe that the information we seek is out there and, like a giant jigsaw puzzle, we have to find the hidden pieces and put it all together. To discover these pieces we will have to search many areas, from cutting-edge scientific information to historical reports and documents, some even seemingly unrelated. We must then look hard at the information available through field investigations and experiments. All of this will bring us closer to the answer.

There are three big questions to examine: Where do ghosts exist? Can we see them? What are the physical attributes of a ghost?

The Environment of Reality

We all thrive within an environment that is suitable to our physiology; for example, we couldn't exist without great technical assistance on Mars. Because we are physical we need certain things, like air, water, food, and sunlight. Our reality is developed through our senses and through the general consensus of those around us. Our perception is built by education, experience, trial and error, and investigation of our surroundings. The binding that holds all this together is our memories and emotions. Without memory we would simply cease to exist. Ghosts exist within their own environment and all the unique elements that combine to allow them to remain and operate just beyond our perception. The study of this unseen environment brings us closer to the spirit world. Is there a place where ghosts walk? Yes, and most of it has been seen and measured. I have read with great interest theories from skeptics like Michael Persinger and Vic Tandy who try to explain away ghostly activity as simple EMF waves or standing waves. They have done tremendous research into their respective fields and have shown wonderful results that do not disprove the existence of ghosts, but rather the opposite. Their work has tapped into the alien environment where ghosts dwell. For ghosts to exist, their reality, like ours, requires many things. Tandy and Persinger are seeing first-hand some of those elements.

There has been a great deal of interesting work in specific areas of science that has explored the various phenomena of ghosts. The unanimous conclusion in all cases was that there is no such thing as ghosts. Being an investigator and researcher in the field of parapsychology, I was naturally intrigued by this research. I began studying other sources of data available and started to piece together this information as it may have applied to the phenomena of ghostly activity. I felt this has shown some promise in opening doors to this mystery. The areas investigated were electromagnetic fields, ion effects and ion wind, infrasound and extremely low frequencies, and the UV light spectrum. I formulated a theory on the last topic through field observations.

Electromagnetic energy exists within each of us. Scientists are now examining this energy at the cellular level, leading to the belief that it is a platform for information communication from one cell to another. Ongoing research is also trying to redefine what death is, as it has been discovered that at the time of brain death there remains communication at the cellular level within the body. Near death researchers have looked at this with great interest, as subjects have reported actions and conversations within hospital emergency and operating rooms after they had been pronounced brain dead, only to be resuscitated. Researchers now feel the information within the body was retained by this energy at the cellular level. Once the individual was revived, they had full knowledge of what had happened while they were dead. This is very exciting on its own; however, if we throw into the equation the fact that energy cannot be destroyed, could this individual energy remain if the body were not revived but pronounced permanently deceased?

The U.S. military is well aware of the energy within the human body and is conducting experiments to harness that power for operations in the field. This new type of bio battery charging system is still in its infant stages. The principle is that the human heart, as it pumps, produces about four watts of energy. This energy flux spirals around our bodies and produces an energy field that can extend up to fifteen feet beyond our bodies. As the military wishes to harness this power to charge communication and GPS battery packs, it opens the window to some speculations. For instance, as this energy field moves around us, it has to touch and come into contact with other energy fields, as demonstrated by the Kirlian effect. Could this interaction allow transference of information, and can this be associated with déjà vu, second sight, and empathic experiences? Most people have unlearned this method of processing information through fear. This would explain the gut feeling people get, which normally is a warning of sorts.

But does this energy truly retain information? In 1939, Semyon Kirlian discovered, by accident, what would eventually be termed the Kirlian effect: a photographic procedure that seems to capture the life force that appears to surround every living thing. It was further noted in Kirlian investigations that changes in moisture could indicate emotional changes, which affect the coronal discharges around the subject. If these photos truly demonstrate the life force, then there seems to be integrity within the memory matrix. This was demonstrated with his famous photo, which shows a leaf with the top portion cut off, although the Kirlian effect shows the aura of the entire leaf.

In 1985, at The Academy of Sciences in Moscow, a scientist was mapping a DNA sample with a laser. He fired the laser into the target chamber but had forgotten to place his specimen slide into the target area. What occurred was an image of the previous DNA sample, as though it were still present within the chamber. The equipment was inspected and further tests were conducted. They all produced the same result; it seemed the laser was being influenced by what is now termed "The DNA Phantom." It was determined that when the sample was removed, something remained, invisible to the human eye, that could influence light waves and leave an imprint. Could the energy signature of DNA leave a signature standing wave in its environment? Could these invisible lines of force be part of the integrity memory matrix?

In quantum physics, quantum coherence means that subatomic particles are able to cooperate with one another. Coherence establishes communication. Particles seem to be aware of each other and are interconnected by bands of electromagnetic fields. Let's imagine for a moment that they operate like a tuning fork and, as information cascades along these lines of electromagnetic fields, they all begin to resonate together. When this occurs, and they move into a phase sync, they all begin acting like one giant wave. It then becomes difficult to tell them apart. If some action is done to one of them, it will affect them all.

In 1923, Russian medical professor Alexander G. Gurvich discovered that DNA is an essential source of light energy in the form of biophotons, or what he termed "mitogenetic rays." These rays exist in every living organism and operate into the ultraviolet spectrum of light. This may also be what produces the aura seen by the Kirlian effect. In this respect, DNA could then, in essence, be the master tuning fork, playing at a particular frequency that would start a cascade of information, which all other particles would fall in line and follow.

Ions are charged atoms; they can be negative (more electrons) or positive (more protons). A negative charge and a positive charge will attract each other, while two negatives or two positives will repel each other. Charged objects will create an electric field around themselves. Ions that become trapped will stay together and may produce a densely packed cloud. The ions within the cloud move by repelling and attracting one another. Ions can be generated in abundance whenever energy is transferred into the air. One method of transference is ultraviolet light. Positive ions can cause heavy, oppressed feelings.

The study of ions and static electricity has produced results that can be studied in a lab and reproduced, including hair standing on end, goosebumps, cold spots, and sensations of being touched. Further, there can be various visual phenomena, such as glowing balls of light. Static discharge can produce snapping, crackling, and banging noises, as well as water from condensation. All these phenomena have been reported in supposed hauntings.

I remember a particular Saturday night when I was conducting an investigation in the *Overshadows* project. I was walking down the hall on the upper floor; the activity in the house was abundant and we were recording at the time. Something, or someone, came out of a room and ran towards me. On impact, it passed through me. My body felt as if it had just been woken up and my blood had just started pumping again. Everything was cold and tingly. Could this entity, running through me, have pulled hundreds or thousands of ions into me, causing this effect?

If we assemble some of the pieces and make a giant leap, we can ask ourselves, What if something of us does survive after death, something that retains intelligence, emotion, and memory? What would it look like? Could it have some of the characteristics we have just discussed and exist as a small ball of invisibility, just beyond our perception? Could this be what Doctor Duncan MacDougall of Haverhill, Massachusetts, observed and reported in his death observation experiments? He reported, in *American Medicine* in April 1907, an unexplainable loss of weight of from 1.5 to 2.5 ounces from his subjects at the time of death. Could this be something of the soul?

However, could an invisible ball of intelligent energy explain tens of thousands of reports of apparitions being seen worldwide? Not likely. So what was the significance of these experiments, and how should we logically proceed?

There seem to be several stages to a ghost's existence; they can be beyond our perception, seen as stringy shadows, or visible as a form of apparition. Let's start with the shadows and how and why we might see them. As I combed through hundreds of reports and articles, patterns and consistencies seemed to emerge. First, I had to understand how the human eye works, which led me to a multitude of medical texts and several doctors and optometrists.

Every person has two types of vision: foveal vision, which is direct and focused, is perfect for seeing details; peripheral vision is suited for detecting shadows. Peripheral vision isn't used often, as we are no longer predators, hunting for food and on guard against attacks from other predators. Our peripheral is designed to allow low-resolution vision and motion detection at 180 degrees at a wide range of illuminations. Foveal uses cones (colour vision), which have filters that prevent a large portion of ultraviolet light from reaching the retina. Peripheral uses rods (black and white vision), which are sensitive to ultraviolet light. In the majority of people the UV filters do not completely filter out all of the UV light, as there are small gaps at the corners of their eyes.

Why Children and Pets Perceive More Phenomena than Adults

The structure and development of the eye has a great deal to do with seeing ghosts. Spirit composition reflects UV light at certain points of the manifestation process, within the UV-A spectrum of 380 to 315 nanometers (nm). UV-A light is the basis of the research, as it is found both indoors and outdoors, whereas UV-B light (314 to 280nm) and UV-C light (279 to 200 nm) are not found indoors, where these phenomena are generally seen.

The UV filters within the human eye develop over time, and with age the lens of the eye hardens and becomes yellow, thus allowing the eye to decrease its absorbing ability, blocking out more UV radiation. UV will enter the eyes of children and infants at full strength.

Dogs have the ability to detect movement in low lighting, and because of their short lifespan they rarely develop the ability to block out UV light.

What does this have to do with ghosts? Let us examine several pieces of this puzzle.

A report was written by Professor Margaret Livingstone of Harvard University regarding Leonardo da Vinci's painting the Mona Lisa, according to the BBC news report of February 18, 2003. Apparently the smile of the Mona Lisa is not visible when it is looked at directly; however, if you look elsewhere on the painting, the smile becomes evident. Professor Livingstone explains that this is a result of the way our eyes process visual information. The smile is painted almost completely in low spatial frequencies, and these are seen best by our peripheral vision.

An article appeared in the *Journal of the Society of Psychical Research* regarding Vic Tandy and the ghost in the machine, Vol. 62, No. 851, April 1998. It reported several instances of sensing and sighting ghostly phenomena. Tandy discovered a standing wave of approximately 19 Hz, and he also noticed that visual input related to the phenomena was always detected by peripheral vision.

There are numerous reports of people relating the same phenomena, which are now being termed "shadow people." This phenomenon is not new. People have often seen black or dark images moving out of the peripheral vision, only to have them disappear when they turn their heads. Is it possible that these shadow people exist in the UV spectrum of light, reflecting UV light waves? When the observer turns to look directly at the image, does the UV filter within the eye instantly block it from perception? Seeing these spirits with their peripheral vision may be why monks in medieval times placed small mirrors up beside their noses.

I began studying several photos of apparitions that were reflected in mirrors. The photos didn't show an apparition in the room, but the reflections clearly showed an image within the mirror. Because in-depth experiments with infrared imaging proved to be extremely poor, I started to look at the other end of visible light — ultraviolet light. This seemed exciting because very little research and exploration has been conducted in the UV spectrum. The camera flash, when fired, flares not only visible light but also UV light. When the UV flare impacts and interacts with a spirit's energy signature it leaves a split-second imprint upon a mirror or reflective surface; this, acting like the emulsions of film, lasts long enough for the camera to capture the image of the spirit's reflection. Similar photos of a completely different nature were taken in the 1940s and 1950s, where the emulsion of the film detected and printed spots or orbs showing otherwise undetectable radioactive isotopes in the atmosphere after nuclear testing. After discussing much of my theory on UV waves and their relationship with spirit energy with team member John Mullan, he summed it up with an analogy: "It is like dust particles floating around the room, you can't see them, but regardless they are still there. When you catch a sunbeam shining in through a window the floating dust is suddenly illuminated."

It was further noted on our surveillance tapes from the house of secrets in Toronto that although there were sounds in the hallway immediately in front of the camera, nothing could be seen directly. However, when the sun peeked in the front room's window there was an immediate reaction and images began to appear. Because we couldn't see in the UV light spectrum, we could not determine exactly what was going on. What we did see were unusual light phenomena: bending around corners, bowing in certain areas, pulsating, and not producing a consistent saturation within the view field. We further observed a strange fog that interacted with the light, sometimes intermingling with it, sometimes pushing it back in spots. Images can be seen within the light and fog, although not clearly. There were also times when the sunlight was clearly coming in the front window while a stronger light came from the opposite direction, pushing the sunlight back out of the hallway.

So what we have is a great deal of information; now we have to try to piece it together to discover what a ghost is and what it looks like. As previously mentioned, there seem to be three stages of existence for these entities: undetectable, shadows, and some form of manifesting apparition. The first is where they exist the majority of the time, a small mass no larger than 2.5 ounces of intelligent energy, just beyond our perception in the ultraviolet spectrum of light. All that remains of its memories, intelligence, and social attributes are contained within a micro electromagnetic field. This field has a resonance of between 6.5 to 7 Hz. This number was derived from field tests and experiments while on ghost investigations and through coordination and cooperation with several paranormal research groups worldwide. The shadowy figures we see are nothing more than interplay of ultraviolet light and the spirit's memory matrix, not unlike the phantom DNA effect.

The Memory Matrix and the Ping-pong Ball

One evening at the house investigated in *Overshadows*, my wife and I had gone over to visit the family when a strange event occurred. Over the course of our visit the daughter of the family suggested we play ping-pong. Everyone agreed, feeling that a little bit of fun would be a good stress relief from the events normally occurring in the house. During the game a wild return of the ball left the table and struck something in open space, something we couldn't see. The ball ricocheted back and forth in what seemed to be a very tight containment field.

After bouncing about ten to twelve times in rapid succession, the ball fell to the floor. It was witnessed by all five of us.

Some things happen completely by accident. It was early morning, around 5:00 a.m., and I was preparing for work. The kettle was on the stove and had come to a boil when I came around the corner from the bathroom to the kitchen. I immediately heard movement at the far end of the kitchen near the stove; it sounded like feet shuffling on the floor. The steam came out of the spout of the kettle, rose straight up about six inches, and quickly dissipated. What I found so intriguing was the appearance of a rogue stream of steam that moved 160 degrees away from the kettle as if it contained something. The rogue steam did not dissipate rapidly like the normal steam, but maintained a fog-like appearance as it crossed the kitchen at a constant height of four and a half feet for five or six seconds before it finally disappeared near the dining room doorway fourteen feet from the stove. It was this observation that led me on to investigate the possibility of a memory matrix. I had to wonder, if the water content of the steam were higher, would a manifestation have occurred?

But How Do They Manifest?

At times in every person's life, emotions can be so intense they may become uncontrollable. I believe the trigger of a physical manifestation is the involuntary production of a negative or positive emotion. These emotions have a strong link to, but are not limited to, the individual's memory. As the individual lives within its own memory, emotionally charged events will come to the surface. Thoughts, memories, or observed occurrences can easily create a dynamic response, even on a subconscious level. How we deal with emotion in life is no different in the afterlife; feelings are formed by experience, opinions, and attitudes. The reaction to them may be extremely powerful and involuntary and may even create behaviour that is questionable and bizarre. One event demonstrating a positive emotion as a trigger was observed when children on a school trip visited an old house set up as a museum to show what life was like in the 1860s. (See "A Call for Help — Oakville.") The original owner (now deceased) had lost a grandchild in 1880. As the children entered the house, the entity saw a child who closely resembled her grandson. The resulting emotion triggered the physical manifestation, and the woman appeared as a ghostly figure to the children. The feeling was not reciprocated, and the children fled the house, screaming.

When an entity has a strong emotion there is a shift within the electromagnetic field, causing it to polarize. When this dielectric field polarizes, it starts a chain reaction. There is an escalation in its normal operating frequency, from 6.5 to 19 Hz. A harmonic resonance from within this field causes a wave to form from the memory matrix. This field begins absorption of materials and energy from within the surrounding environment. The absorbed materials become coherent and oscillate in harmony. This starts to produce the exact configuration of what the entity looked like in life, as demonstrated by the Kirlian effect and the phantom DNA effect. UV wavelengths cause ion radiation that knocks electrons from atoms, causing them to become highly reactive, beginning the formulation of a lattice structure. This lattice vibrates in the infrasound spectrum at approximately 4 Hz.

As the material is pulled in from the proximity of the event, a thermal void develops within the area, leaving cold spots. A partial form may start to appear. Depending on its intensity more of the form may begin to be produced. If the emotional event is terminated, the manifestation will quickly dissipate. Depending on how long the manifestation maintains its form, the observation of auditory static discharge may be heard. As well, pools of cold water may appear as condensation forms.

The amount of material collected from the surrounding environment will dictate the type of manifestation. Limited material may allow only a fog charged with ions. There may be light phenomena associated with this fog, due to the charged particles. Within low energy, long-wave ultraviolet light, photons may be captured by electrons that are orbiting the nuclei of atoms. As they gain energy, they become boosted to excited states. As the electrons return to the lower energy state there is a release of energy in the form of visible light. This light energy can be passed from one molecule to another.

Additional material will allow for more complex structures, ranging from a partial formation of the head and/or torso right up to a solid body manifestation.

Depending on the structure and the ability to allow information to cascade within the structure (e.g. telekinesis, the true sense of the phrase "Mind over matter"), this would allow for manipulation and would dictate the varying movements of the structure, as reported by witnesses. The movement may vary from a rigid form that seems to be unable to move, to what is termed a glider, right up to full animation.

Water's Role in Building the Matrix

Water molecules seem simple, consisting of two hydrogen atoms and one oxygen atom. However, there are many anomalous properties and complexities associated with water molecules, and without this molecule, all life would cease to exist.

It is interesting to observe that as water molecules interact with ultraviolet radiation there is excitation and absorption of protons at approximately 266 nm. As this occurs the frequency range is expanded, causing the molecules to move, stretch, and bend, which generates heat. This raises them to higher frequencies, creating more heat; this thermal motion allows the molecule to react to electromagnetic fields.

Water is dipolar and can be aligned by electrostatic fields; it can also be influenced by magnetic fields. These influences can increase hydrogen bonding strength and produce interactions between water molecule clusters, allowing ordered structures to be built at the molecular level. Because water has a high dielectric constant it works as a solvent for the absorption of other ions; this can cause thermal motion separating the ions within the solution. As the heat from the thermal motion increases, the water molecule dielectric constant decreases, allowing ions to partition, which increases the density value. This is a small but important part of the memory matrix. Biologist Jacques Benveniste is working on a new theory that water molecules have memory and can communicate with one another. His experiments suggest that we will one day be able to record and then listen to these communications between molecules. Each type of molecule has its own frequency.

Benveniste explains that the communication happens like a radio broadcast transmitting information to a receiver specifically tuned to that frequency. Water molecules are key because they provide the communication relay. As specific molecules are dissolved, they produce an agitation, which is the release of the encoded message of that molecule. The agitation is detected by absorption by water molecules and transmitted along a chain reaction at the speed of light to a receptive molecule, which creates the action.

Ghostly activity is greatly increased on stormy days and even more so in the winter months. At these times there is an abundance of required elements to assist the spirit to manifest — moisture and static electricity. This may also help to explain why ghostly activity is focused close to water sources like bathrooms.

It may be of interest to note that in 1867, Lord Kelvin discovered that dripping water, like that found in a leaky faucet in your tub or sink, produces static electricity. This was demonstrated in his experiment "Kelvin's thunderstorm."

The Memory Bubble

Where do ghosts exist? This is a complex question; to understand where they exist we have to rephrase the question to be more accurate. When do ghosts exist? To understand this we have to step out of what we perceive as reality. They exist all around us; the point is, in what time frame? I term this "the memory bubble."

A memory bubble is a reality created by an individual spirit, in which it exists. The bubble matrix consists of a period in time and space, familiar to the individual when they were living. The time it represents is out of sync with real time. The fabric that formulates a memory bubble is frequency, resonating at a specific harmonic value. Each bubble has its own value. It has been discovered that in near death experiences there are common events that occur and are reported. The first is a noise, like a buzzing sound, which could actually be the change in frequency from this reality to the next reality. The next is the feeling of losing track of time. People then report they enter a life review, normally following a chronology from birth to death. The phrase "My life flashed before my eyes" is an appropriate statement within this context. This process can last up to three days and is part of the memory bubble development. Had they not been resuscitated, I believe these individuals would have chosen a slice of time from their life reviews, and that time frame would have then become their new realities. Their realities contain all the things that one would find in this reality — sight, sound, furniture, and people, living and deceased — and because the mental attributes are intact they also retain humility, the reason why naked ghosts are rarely seen. The selection will, of course, have a deep personal meaning. It may range from an extremely happy time, to something they obsessed over, to something they did or had done to them.

In the event of a traumatic death, such as murder or accident or a soldier in combat, the very fact that the event was so horrific may create a memory that supercedes all other memories, holding them to the place of death. It could be that they do not quite understand what has happened to them, or that they don't like the outcome of the original event that caused their death, and they may feel that it is possible to change what occurred.

The memory bubble may not represent life exactly as it was when they were living, but rather as they perceived it to be. The entire bubble resonates at a frequency beyond our perception, and we are surrounded by these bubbles everywhere we go. Most are silent and exist in harmony, never to be known by us. However, there are, at times, rare situations when these bubbles make themselves known to us in various ways. There are two specific triggers that allow this to happen. The first is when a spirit focuses on an important event or problem in their past life. This intense focus raises the spirit's emotional energy level and therefore raises the amplitude of the frequency, which allows paranormal sights, sounds, and smells to manifest in our reality. The second trigger is a highly emotionally charged memory, which causes deep thought, turmoil, and disturbance to the spirit. Roving smells is one phenomenon that transcends the boundaries of both realities. Another is the sound of moving furniture and breaking objects, when there is no evidence to suggest anything has been broken or moved. They are simply reverberating out of their memory and into our reality, at a resonance we can process. Major disturbances come when the spirit perceives either a chance to communicate with the living, to manipulate your choices and actions to produce a result they wish to see occur, or an opportunity to avoid threat by you to them in changing something they do not want changed or learning something they do not want you to know about their past.

The modification and expansion of a memory bubble occurs when more than one spirit in close proximity share a specific time frame. An example would be where many people died in a single event such as war. They rely on each other's memory information of that time and adapt the information to the bubble, causing the bubble to expand. (For more information, please see the section on clusters in this chapter.)

How a Living Individual and a Spirit Meet

The spirit is outside of our perception, existing within its memory bubble; occasionally something occurs that serves to synchronize the two realities, allowing them to collide in time and space. If you remember having a dream where a sound around you, possibly a clock radio going off, was incorporated into your dream instead of waking you up, it will give you a better understanding of what is taking place. This synchronicity occurs when the spirit memory perceives a living individual as part of its memory bubble, due to a resemblance or a simple convenience, causing the spirit to come forward to inter-act and emotions to escalate. It is at this point of interaction that the two realities collide. The living individual becomes terrified, and the spirit, realizing this person is not part of their reality, quickly retreats back beyond our perception.

Memory Bubble Development — What It Represents to the Individual, and What It Means with Regards to Judgment Day

I understand that religion can be an extremely delicate subject. Everyone has, or should have, the freedom to follow and practise the religion of their choice. Regardless of the particular religion, they all have the same principal messages for all of us:

1. Be good to one another and take care of those around us.

2. Believe in and worship God.

Now, having said that, I have to tread into the deeper water of what all religions consider a day of judgment. There are common links regarding this event between Judeo-Christian and Islamic teachings. The top of the list is that they all agree that there will be such a day.

The memory bubble is developed out of the individual's memory, memories consisting of events, emotions, and experience. People are, believe it or not, their own harshest critic and they will, without knowing, put themselves where they need to be.

Heaven is a place where the individual has died, accepted and acknowledged their sins in life, and found an enjoyable place in time where they were most happy in life. The memory bubble is then formed around that time, transferring them to an existence of peaceful harmony. These entities are quiet.

Hell is a place where the individual has died and is obsessing over things they had done, or that had been done to them — over money, property, or a relationship. They try to make people understand that they were victims or are hiding a crime. They virtually transform themselves into an undying hell, where the memory bubble they create contains all the sins and fears that haunted them in life. These entities are restless and active, and while some may be malevolent, others may be benevolent.

These two places are temporary until the final day of judgment, when all will be collected and brought forth, along with the living, for judgment.

In 1999 Pope John Paul II spoke to an audience in Rome about what Heaven and Hell were. He stated that neither was a physical place, but rather what the individual made of them, more states of thought.

Clusters

After weeks of constant electronic surveillance of the *Overshadows* house we finally got it — video footage to substantiate what I was theorizing all along, what I now term a cluster.

This can be described as the state wherein several entities merge together and become fully integrated into each other, without losing their individual identities. There does, however, seem to be a hierarchy within the cluster. They demonstrate intelligence and the ability to reason, plan, calculate, manipulate, and communicate.

Clusters appear to assemble through either social or antisocial behaviour, meaning the individual can agree to enter the cluster or be forced into and absorbed by the cluster. Once an individual is brought into the cluster, the knowledge of all within that unit becomes available for the unit to draw upon. The bigger the cluster, the more knowledge and power they will exhibit. Keep in mind that the most up-to-date knowledge that they will share is from the most recently deceased who has been brought into the cluster. For example, if the last entity to enter the cluster had died in the 1940s, then that cluster would not have any knowledge of equipment, advancements, or information beyond the 1940s.

Each cluster normally has a principal entity that draws on the power of the unit to manifest. The cluster can be separated briefly, but there remains some unseen tether that pulls them back together. The cluster can be shattered through forced interaction and communication; however, this causes a dangerous realignment of power within the unit, as it seems there is a careful balance of malevolent and benevolent forces. It may be interesting to note that in all cases with which I have been involved there has never been just one entity. (Although it is important to remember that not all hauntings involve a cluster; there are situations and locations with only one entity.) The balance of benevolent and malevolent forces, be it by accident or design, seems to set out rules for them. Each action will have an equal and opposite reaction; for example, if one would help us the other would then be given the opportunity to hurt us, and vice versa. Neither wants the other to have the upper hand, so there is an automatic stalemate. This also applies to communication as it may be considered helpful and could bring on some sort of retaliation.

Imagine that an individual dies, returns to his or her childhood home, and encounters other entities.

ENCOUNTERS CLUSTER

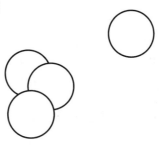

IS DRAWN INTO CLUSTER

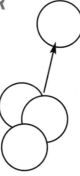

MERGES WITH CLUSTER

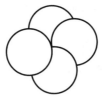

It was noted on the videotape that the cluster manifested as an incandescent light with an ambient fog. The entities within appeared to orbit or rotate around one another, pushing individually to the surface, each taking a turn. Although stationary, the entities within moved with startling speed, in short, jerky movements.

Observation of the cluster: there seemed to be an unexplainable loud bang, which announced that the event or observable scene was about to change. This bang should not be confused with what I have termed the "ticking noise," which has been recorded. On many occasions the ticking sound on EVP is believed to be information, so low in frequency it cannot be fully developed by our equipment.

In all cases of subjective surveillance of places believed to be haunted, data shows that not only were they aware of the equipment in operation, they interfered with it and reacted with anger. It seemed that 60 Hz electromagnetic fields generated by the equipment caused them some problems. This may be due to their lower frequency fields.

Removing or rescuing an entity from a cluster is extremely dangerous. When an entity is told to leave an area by someone tasked to clear a home or other building, communication is established with a receptive benevolent entity. By their nature, cooperation comes easily and they leave. The person reports the job completed. The balance is devastated, and the malevolent entities now gain power, thus resulting in increased harmful or destructive activity.

We have experienced this many times through our investigations. Our psychic kept telling us that he was having difficulties with communication, due to what he was describing as "a bag of ghosts." It seemed that the one in charge would silence the others.

We discussed this problem and formulated a plan of action: a small psychological game would be played with the one in charge. We went back to the house and attempted to establish communication. As usual, everything started out smoothly, but after a couple of minutes communication was cut off. We then told the malevolent entity that something he would find unacceptable was taking place elsewhere on the property. At that point two things occurred: first, communication restarted; second, the people at the location we had mentioned saw a large black shadow manifesting, along with loud noises of banging and furniture moving.

We wanted to further understand this phenomenon, so we had to take our equipment on the road. We first chose a house where a lot of preliminary investigative work had been conducted. We started communication, and again, after a few minutes, we were faced with nothing more than gibberish. The malevolent entity was addressed and told to leave temporarily. We were working in the basement at the time and we heard the heavy footfalls on the main floor above our heads, followed by the back door being slammed shut, as if letting us know it was gone. Communication recommenced immediately.

The next location was a large tourist attraction, which had a documented history of hauntings. Here, the principal force would not leave and would not allow the others to communicate.

People put incredible abilities on the spirit world; it is we who have complicated our understanding of what they are. Simply put, they are those dearly departed souls who continue their existence in the afterlife. They are who they have always been, just removed from their bodily form. They go about their business, living in a memory bubble collectively created by them and those around them. Where it becomes complicated is the way we think of reality. We know what it means to us in this life, but when we cross over the boundary into the afterlife it becomes alien to us. There is no time per se, but rather a time period. For example, if the entity existed and died within the 1940s, then the period would be the 1940s. If a transient entity decided to join the first entity and was from the 1970s, then their time period would be expanded to include the 1940s to the 1970s, and they would be able to communicate information from within those time periods to one another. This would allow for the expansion of the memory bubble that they maintain and exist within.

The cluster appears to produce a narrow field time shift; this bubble envelops them and moves with them. However, if the cluster contains many entities the bubble grows as well. In some cases it can extend beyond the group and it is possible for someone living to pass into and through this bubble and experience a time shift. For example, in 1901 there was a case involving two English women, Anne Moberley and Eleanor Jourdain, who, on a trip to Paris, reported that while walking the ground of Versailles they seemed to walk into the past. They saw people in period dress from the late eighteenth century, around the time of Marie Antoinette, and reported that the environment around them had changed, feeling heavy, depressed, and very unpleasant.

Within this bubble a spirit's thought processes, if traumatic and powerful, may manifest into our reality, and should one spirit be reinforced with others, its thoughts could take on a life of their own. The manifestation can separate from the memory bubble and form its own reality. This would explain the sightings of ghostly ships and trains, most of which suffered some devastating fate in history. That manifestation bubble which has detached and is not supported seems real, but quickly dissipates without warning and is gone from the witness's view.

More Questions than Answers — Becoming Philosophical

Recently a group of us went to Fort George, located at Niagara-on-the-Lake, for an investigation. Dee, Anita, and Krystal had been there previously and had the great fortune of capturing the image of a soldier inside the tunnel located near the powder magazine. This tunnel represented an important question to me, so I was very excited to go on this trip and see it for myself.

That evening we assembled at the fort and ventured to the tunnel. Dee immediately sensed spirit energy inside the tunnel and told us a person named Joseph was present. At first he was curious about not only why we were there but also who we were. It wasn't until Dee made it clear that we were Canadian that he settled down.

It seems, from this photograph and the information collected independently by other research groups, that the spirits here are soldiers and that they are within their memory bubble and continue to function in this bygone era, preparing to fight in the War of 1812. They are as they were in that time and they see the fort and surrounding area as it was back then. Where the excitement comes in for me is that they are seen in the tunnel, a tunnel that wasn't built until 1965. The tunnel shouldn't exist to them or be part of their memory bubbles. It now seems possible that not only an individual's memory but also the historic memory of an entire place can be altered.

Could this mean that having access to the tunnel gives them a tactical advantage over the advancing American forces, who would not know of it? And if the existence of alternate timelines is a reality, would this now change the historical outcome of this battle? Further, could introducing other changes to an environment modify other memory bubbles? Maybe there is a way for an investigator to use this information to their advantage in field experiments.

I brought this question up to the group and the consensus was that some entities were conscious of their situation and what was going on around them in our timeline. In other words, they knew that they were deceased, knew relatively what year it was, and could understand the current changes in their environment. There were also those who were not conscious of their situation and had no idea that they were dead or that anything had changed around them. For these individuals the place continued to exist as it was in their time. It would, then, be the conscious ones who could use this tunnel.

A little girl who has been seen in the fort and who is believed to be the young daughter of one of the officers who served there used to come to the entrance of the tunnel but would never enter. Many people in several paranormal groups have reported this girl at the opening of the tunnel. It has been recently noticed that this girl will now enter and use the tunnel. Could this be part of the expansion of the memory bubble, wherein she has been made aware of this tunnel by those entities that are conscious and now has the information of our timeline to enter and see the tunnel as it is?

I have made observations of both people in the field who were part of an investigation and psychics applying their skill while conducting an investigation. I at first found it very curious that some sort of contact was made, be it audio or visual, at times when the participants were in a relaxed state. Even the psychics, prior to attempting to make contact, tried to move into a relaxed mindset. I went back to question many of those who had reported this type of communication phenomena and although each one described entirely different situations, they all stated they were in a relaxed state of mind prior to the event. The change occurred during the event itself: the subject would move from a relaxed state of mind towards anxiety and panic and the event would quickly dissipate. Psychics, however, would maintain contact.

I started to review hundreds of reports, trying to find an exception to this observation, yet I could not. Every case I read put the subject in a routine, relaxed situation prior to the event. This led me back to my earlier theory, that when the subject's brainwave patterns lower to the alpha pattern of between 8 and 13 Hz per second there is an increased chance of becoming involved in some of these phenomena, and the chances increase even more as the subject's brainwave patterns lower into the theta state of 4 to 7 Hz. The more the subject's brain patterns lowered, the closer they became to the frequency of the deceased. The reverse would, of course, hold true as well — anxiety and panic would push the subject's brainwave patterns up into the beta pattern of 14 to 30 Hz, and this would ultimately terminate the sensory connection causing the event to end.

Statistically, why do women see ghostly phenomenon more than men? The answer may be all in the brain. Women are generally more intuitive when it comes to understanding and sensing others' emotional distress, pain, and suffering. Observe a mother with a newborn baby — there is no verbal communication, but the mother will instinctively know what the child requires. It could be this link that allows the attachment and the perception of an event of great emotional importance occurring close by.

MRI tests show activity in the brain, specifically within the region known as the cingulate gyrus (the emotional control centre), is higher within females. The female brain secretes higher levels of the hormones oxytocin and serotonin. It is interesting to note that serotonin produces a calming effect.

Intuition could very well be a byproduct of the ability of the brain to perceive external emotional energy; couple this ability with a higher level of serotonin and you have all the elements for an encounter with spirit energy.

Studying how and why communication may occur is important for the investigator, especially if we plan on developing new technology for that express purpose. It is, however, interesting to note other problems encountered by people with psychic ability. Having worked with several psychics I have heard them run into difficulties while trying to tune into a particular event on an investigation. The problem they report is always the same: trying to sort through layers of time. Imagine that you have a book that contains the entire history of everyone in your family, going back a dozen generations; however, the information is not written in chronological order but rather randomly throughout the book. Now, imagine that someone felt that some of the information was more important than the rest, so they duplicated specific pages and inserted them here and there. This seems to be what most psychics are faced with in the field. Trying to sort out the details from a haunted site is no easy task, as there may be multiple spirits all screaming information at you, wanting their story known. The psychic has the difficult task of trying to sort out what information belongs where, and at what time period. The important clue here is why so many ghosts can inhabit the same place. It seems that they are separated by the boundary of time. These partitions in time all resonate with a slight variation in frequency, keeping them on the fringe of one another's perception. The length of these partitions is unknown. They do seem to be linked by memory, not specifically the memory of someone, but rather the memory of actually having met the person first-hand. There is, however, evidence to suggest that these partitions can be breached or expanded to include those who have recently died, possibly because the gap within the frequency variation widens at ninety- or one-hundred-year intervals and the narrow field allows for transference. This may explain the exception to the rule wherein the spirit of a recently deceased person may come into contact with someone unknown to them, simply because of the narrow field of the frequency and the common location. This seemed evident in one of my investigations where a recently deceased girl ran into a spirit who had died in the late 1940s. They were able to interact with each other, but neither of them was aware of Mrs. Best, who resided on the same property and had died in the early nineteenth century.

The Ghost Animal

In several investigations there were questions raised by investigators and those who requested assistance regarding the spirits of animals haunting a particular place. Observations and EVP, in a lot of these instances, showed they were there: something small jumping up on the bed, nails moving on the hardwood floor, scratching, and barking, growling, or meowing. But are they really there? This question is an extremely difficult one, simply because, as an investigator, there is no way one could establish any meaningful communication with a spirit animal to either confirm or deny their existence. There are a great number of EVP recordings that clearly indicate their attendance at the haunting. But is this proof? At a previous investigation, I was running constant surveillance on the house and had several tapes that indicated both a dog and a cat were present. The house was empty and controlled. The recording level supported that they were in close proximity to the equipment. I also captured, on the audiotape, a girl and a woman speaking. The conversation was later verified as having taken place the previous year, prior to the tape being made. The woman and both animals were confirmed to be very much alive, but the girl was deceased. The woman whose voice was recorded was the girl's mother; the cat and dog belonged to the family when they lived in that house. So were the animals' spirits there? No. My only conclusion at this time has to be that the girl's spirit manifested a memory of that event, which included her living mother and pets. Do I suggest that there are no animal spirits? Certainly not. However, to date, I have no evidence to substantiate their existence.

As for us, the living, we assume much. For example, we assume that we are in real time — the present. However, when we have a simple conversation, how far out of sync with the present are we? You meet a person and want to greet them; you formulate a message in your mind and then relay it. It travels from you through the air by waves to them, passes through their ear, the frequencies are captured, interpreted, and sent to their brain, where they are processed. Then they formulate a response and the entire process starts again. The amount of time to do all this seems insignificant, but any time delay removes us from real time, moving us out of the present and into the past.

We don't even understand where we fit in, in the great expanse of reality. We assume that we are in the present, all behind us is the past, and just ahead of us is the future.

But what is present time, or real time?

All types of reality coexist, separated by a membrane of frequency. Once we begin to access the frequencies just behind us and just ahead of us, we will be able to use these for a jump-off base, to dig even further into our past and also into our future. We can gain a glimpse of these, as these realities are so close to our time reality that like any close proximity frequencies, there is interference or overlapping and we associate them with ghosts, déjà vu, or psychic phenomena.

Reality Matrix

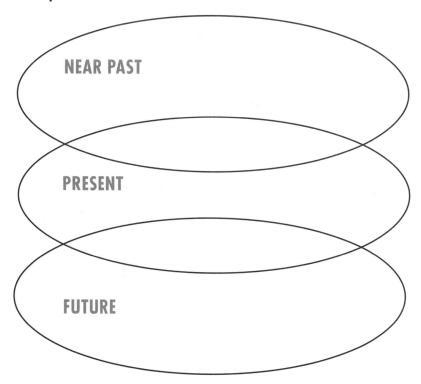

We can think of ourselves as tuned in to a simple radio station; it's a wonderful station, and it has everything, so much variety. One day something happens and we discover another radio station. It's close by, but we can't seem to tune it in clearly, although every once in a while we get little bits and pieces of information. Nothing concrete, just enough to let us know that they are there.

MANIFESTATION CHART

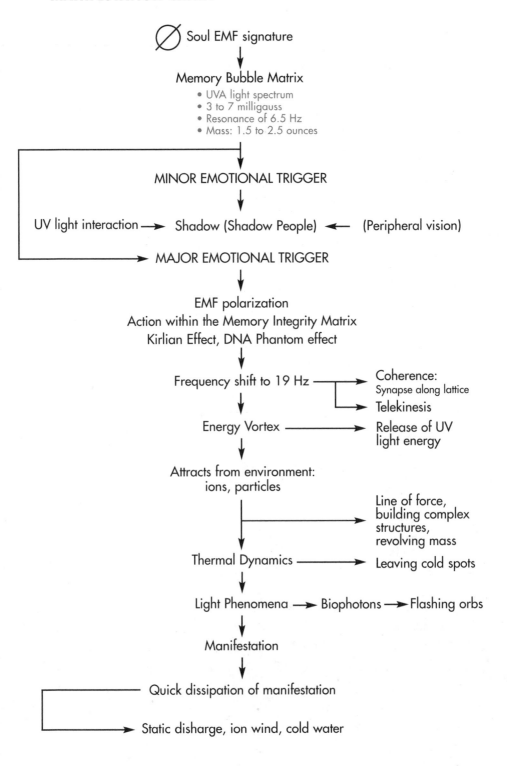

Soul EMF signature

Memory Bubble Matrix
- UVA light spectrum
- 3 to 7 milligauss
- Resonance of 6.5 Hz
- Mass: 1.5 to 2.5 ounces

MINOR EMOTIONAL TRIGGER

UV light interaction → Shadow (Shadow People) ← (Peripheral vision)

MAJOR EMOTIONAL TRIGGER

EMF polarization
Action within the Memory Integrity Matrix
Kirlian Effect, DNA Phantom effect

Frequency shift to 19 Hz → Coherence:
Synapse along lattice
→ Telekinesis

Energy Vortex → Release of UV light energy

Attracts from environment: ions, particles

→ Line of force, building complex structures, revolving mass

Thermal Dynamics → Leaving cold spots

Light Phenomena → Biophotons → Flashing orbs

Manifestation

Quick dissipation of manifestation

→ Static discharge, ion wind, cold water

The Investigation Guide

It has always amazed me what we determine to be evidence, depending on the topic. If we are talking about criminal activity, then electronic evidence such as security monitoring devices, which indicate an action occurring in a specific place, as well as surveillance systems that show us what occurred in that location can provide a strong case. Couple this information with witness testimony and the evidence may end in a criminal conviction, even with the absence of DNA samples. However, we may have all of these same elements in a spirit investigation, and yet because the topic is the paranormal, the evidence is automatically dismissed. Information is, for the most part, a piece of a much larger puzzle. Each piece waits for another to reinforce what the first piece has suggested. When this occurs, they call it proof.

The unblinking eye of the camera watches, unafraid, standing its ground where man would flee in terror. A plain, unremarkable white hallway sprawls out in front of its view, and a dim 40-watt light in a white dome hangs from the ceiling. The windows are all blacked out, ensuring there are no outside light sources. Three hours, eighteen minutes of nothing, then something starts to happen. A light starts to grow in the centre of the hall, hardly noticeable at first, more of a glare or reflection. As it starts to expand outward, like a corona, there are small flashing orbs, which move away from it. The light soon extends to the floor and ceiling and touches both walls. It is dense and has a greyish tinge to it, and there appear to be slightly darker shapes moving within it. The light begins to fill the hall; moving towards the camera, finally stopping at the doorway, squeezing into the frame, but not encroaching into the room. There is no reflection or light change within the room at all. It looks like a void in space, and you feel as though if you were to step into the light you would end up in another time or place. After twenty minutes the void starts to recede back down the hall, shrinking into a small ball of light in the centre of the hall, then finally vanishing altogether.

This was the product of three weeks of surveillance work. Sounds exciting, but remember, the camera must record twenty-four hours a day, seven days a week. The investigator has to change the tapes every eight hours. Then the fun starts. Each camera produces one tape; the more cameras, the more tapes. Each tape has to be carefully reviewed and scrutinized by the investigator. Now imagine watching a few hundred hours of tape, with nothing more than a plain, unremarkable white hallway in its view. If you can do this without reaching for the fast forward button, then you may be cut out to do surveillance work.

Ghost investigations sound like fun. What more could you ask for in the way of excitement? Going off to a reputed haunted house in the dead of night with a few friends … However, true investigative work is just that — work. It is long hours of historical research: going to archives and libraries, scanning miles of old newspapers, searching out the history of the house and property, interviewing people, making a preliminary tour to look for rational explanations. Then, when all this is done, there comes the trip to the house for the investigation, which could end up being nothing more than hours of silent boredom with poor results. This doesn't include the costs, which come directly from your own pocket: research, photocopies, travel expenses, equipment, audiotapes, videotapes, batteries, and of course, the big one — your time. So why do we do what we do? Simply put, the mystery remains and there are those of us who have an unquenchable desire to solve it. The satisfaction comes by way of a fascinating photograph of something unexplained, or that disembodied voice on the tape that has just answered one of your questions. To most investigators the question of life after death has clearly been solved for them; they will tell you they know the answer, but they will also tell you it isn't enough for them to know, they want you to know as well.

An investigator has to know a little bit about a lot of things: physics, general science, electronics, human psychology, physiology, history, parapsychology, paranormal theory, photography, how sound works, how light works, investigative techniques, report writing, and the workings of all equipment you may have to use, to name a few.

During an investigation the investigator should maintain meticulous notes and attempt to use some form of scientific method, from start to finish. Standardize a format that can be used to ensure the problem you are required to solve is clearly understood. Be sure to define the basis of the problem; collecting background and historic information on this question will assist you in obtaining a deeper understanding of the task at hand. After gathering and analyzing all available information related to the problem, you will be able to build and announce a hypothesis.

The most difficult task you will face in this research is to develop tests and field experiments of your hypothesis, to see if they can solve the problem. You will have to develop procedures and controls of all your tests and record all the data obtained, including any samples collected, duration of tests and events, occurring phenomena, and observable intervals. Explore any possible alternatives.

Record in a logical manner any predictions that you have made regarding the study of the problem and develop your final conclusion based on the complete analysis of all the data, including any patterns or trends. Separate the data into quantitative (measured instrument data) and qualitative (observable data).

Ensure that all your notes are complete and informative. Does your data support your hypothesis, and is it convincing? Regardless of the answer, explain in detail why. Remember, an investigator has an obligation to report the truth; the evidence of the collected data should tell the story of what is occurring and what the final solution to the problem is. Never jump to conclusions.

Primary Inspection

After interviewing the primary person who has called you in to report the events, you must thoroughly inspect the property to establish a clear understanding of what may have occurred. The first order is to examine every avenue in an attempt to rule out what it was not. It cannot be classified as a true paranormal phenomenon until everything naturally occurring has been eliminated.

Should your preliminary inspection find no natural cause for the phenomenon and the decision be made to continue with a full investigation, then you should set up all witness interview dates.

Interviewing Witnesses

When taking statements, never assume anything. Don't just pull out a notepad or tape recorder; put the witness at ease, ask their permission to record the interview, tell them you want to get what they have to say correctly recorded. Demonstrate that what they have to say is important to you.

Never rush them or show any disbelief in what they are saying. Be a good listener.

Never attempt to lead a witness in any direction, and don't assist them by adding words to their statement or writing your own interpretation. Don't offer your opinion. Let them explain the events in their own words. Show interest, create confidence, and encourage them to talk openly.

Interview witnesses separately. First, use the planned list of questions and get them out of the way. Then ask them to describe the events in their own words; this will allow them to do most of the talking and elaborate on details the questionnaire may have missed.

If you are going to use a tape recorder for recording the interview, ensure you know how to operate the device. Conduct a test to ensure proper volume.

If several witness statements are to be recorded it is best to use a single tape, or group of tapes, for each witness. Write the witness's name and date on each cassette, as well as recording this information at the beginning of each tape.

Aside from the tape recorder, use a notebook to write down further questions during the interview, items that may require further detail or clarification. Don't interrupt the interview; wait until they are finished, then ask your questions. When asking questions use plain English, staying away from technical words and jargon.

Remember, time is a critical factor, as details will diminish. Highlight variations or differences from witness to witness. Keep in mind, most people are not trained observers and therefore see things differently from one another. Most will not remember minor details but rather focus on the event and will normally attach an emotion to it, such as sadness or fright.

Encourage the witness to speak only about information that they themselves heard or saw and not information that they have been told about.

Never interrupt a witness, unless they begin to discuss information irrelevant to the investigation.

Where there are long pauses and the witness is unsure how to proceed, ask questions that will require more than simple yes or no answers.

If the witness has a hard time explaining details, they may be able to provide you with a drawing or sketch. They may also produce photos. If this occurs, make reference to them on the recording and at a later time see if you can obtain copies to attach to your report.

If the witness is willing and you have permission, go to the location of the event and conduct the interview there. This may allow them to be more descriptive and will also give you a better insight as to what occurred and where. The surroundings may also stimulate their memory.

Drawing Out the Area

Do a quick drawing of the area. Have someone assist you with measurements. Draw the floor plan, naming rooms and showing stairs, doors and direction of swing, windows, and forced air vents or radiators. Indicate if there are any air conditioners located in any of the windows, and whether there are any fans, either movable or ceiling mounted. Mark water pipes, and indicate hot or cold. Show lighting locations, and note whether they are fixed to wall, mounted on the ceiling, or a portable lamp. Note the type of floor surfaces (tile, hardwood, carpet, etc.). Draw in anything else of interest. Note any structural changes or modifications from your research.

Setting up a Command Area

Establish an area far enough away from the target site so that it will not interfere with the investigation. This area will be your staging area and will be used for meetings, conversations, smoking, eating, and planning. All surplus equipment will be kept in this area.

Daylight Inspection of Target Area

You should make every effort to inspect and map the area you intend to investigate during daylight hours. This will allow you to do several important tasks while you have the advantage of bright natural light.

1. Map and draw the area.
2. Mark safety hazards; cordon them off with rope or caution tape if necessary.
3. Take and record all of your electronic and atmospheric base line readings and take control photos.

Team Operations and Assignments

Formulate a plan of operation prior to arriving at the site. Each person should have a task assignment from the following list.

1. Observation and data collection.
2. Equipment and data collection.
3. Photo / video records.

Large teams can be reduced to two-person mini teams to cover larger areas. Each team has to know and understand what everyone else is doing; you don't want people using an EMF gauss meter near people doing EVP work, and you don't want flash photography near people using night vision.

Set a time to meet and compare notes. Know who will be assigned to collect, analyze, and compile all data from the investigation.

Videotaping versus Surveillance

Videotaping allows you to follow the movements of team members and any action that may occur. It also allows you to bring the camera to areas of specific interest fairly quickly. Surveillance allows a target area to be monitored and recorded, while removing all human influences.

It has been noted that upon the introduction of audio/video equipment, the first three days are extremely crucial in haunted properties not previously investigated. It seems the investigator can catch activity more consistently as the energies within the property are off guard and not suspecting the introduction of surveillance. After three days, they become aware of the equipment and its purpose and become camera shy. At this time, audio surveillance will increase in activity. A method employed by Paul is to use a camera set at the furthest point from a target area that has shown the highest amount of activity and, over a period of days, even weeks, to move the camera closer to the point of activity. This attempt to herd the energies into a specific area has been very successful in several of our investigations. The most important element for the investigator is having the time necessary to carry out this procedure. Too many times we are rushed, normally due to the property being inhabited and people being unwilling to go through daily routines within the surveillance area. They also don't want to deal with disruptions by the investigator, who must arrive to check equipment and change tapes on a regular basis. Properties that have been previously investigated pose a more difficult task to the team as the energies are guarded and aware that you will attempt to capture their activity on audio and/or video equipment. They become even more covert.

SURVEILLANCE TIPS

- Map the area to be kept under surveillance.
- Have a good understanding of the method and particulars of the reported phenomena.
- Set cameras to monitor target areas. If possible, have cameras overlap view areas, keeping opposing camera in view.
- Check camera views on monitors and adjust as required.
- Run a short fifteen-second recording test on each VCR to ensure proper operation.

- Turn off all monitors, and remove them if possible.
- Set up tape recording equipment in desired locations.
- Ensure all windows and doors are closed. Turn off all non-essential electrical appliances and equipment.
- Have all personnel leave the area.
- Set all devices to record and leave the area yourself.
- Secure the exit.
- Wait for the predetermined amount of time to lapse.
- Note any external noises (car horns, dogs barking, aircraft, etc.) that may affect your recordings.
- Enter and retrieve tapes. Set fresh tapes or, if investigation is complete, remove all equipment.

Safety

It is very important to maintain safety standards while pursuing an investigation. The security of your team is paramount.

SAFETY TIPS

- Never go on an investigation alone.
- Never agree to go on an investigation or meet people you've had contact with through only the telephone or the Internet and whose identity you cannot confirm.
- Always let someone know where you are going and who you will be meeting, as well as when you expect to return.
- Always work with a team of people you know and trust.
- Take a cellphone; ensure the battery is fully charged.
- Take at least two flashlights, with spare batteries.
- Bring a first aid kit.
- When entering a dwelling to conduct an investigation, always have an emergency exit plan.
- Use extreme caution while in and around abandoned properties. Be aware of potential hazards: rotten floors,

broken stairs, homeless people, and teens who may be drinking or using drugs.

- Always obtain permission to enter private property.
- Let the local police know you will be working at the location.

Searching for Sources of Information

Once you have started your investigation you will be looking for sources of information on the property as well as people who may have lived and worked there. Start your search within the community and seek out long-time neighbours. Check with local churches and senior citizen buildings, as these people may remember past events and people within your search area.

You may wish to search the Internet for local folklore and see if there is any previously reported activity at the location you are investigating or in the surrounding area. Places that may provide background information or any existing photographs include your local library, old city directories (phone books), obituaries, and newspaper reports. A lot of the time there will be articles in the local society pages and under local news. Most large newspaper publications will provide a search service. Other sources can be found at local, provincial, and federal archives, genealogy societies, local historical societies, legion halls, taxation offices, and city plan and permit offices.

The Equipment

When using scientific equipment to detect anomalous events in an investigation, it is extremely important to do a thorough inspection of the area prior to the investigation. Map the area and record all your baseline readings on the map. If at all possible, conduct these tests twice, at different times, to establish what may be normal for the target area.

Electronic voice phenomenon is an attempt to record spirit sounds and voices on tape. Many investigators report success in their attempts. The key is to capture a specific piece of information, for example, information that is specifically linked to the property you are investigating or a direct answer to one of your questions. These recordings are harder for the skeptic to dismiss, unlike random words that may be picked up from any number of sources.

There are two methods of recording EVP. The first is to keep the recorder with you and ask specific questions, allowing two minutes to receive an answer. The other method is to try to locate the equipment in an area you believe to be active, close all windows and doors to reduce interference from outside sources, and leave the area, letting the equipment record on its own.

When recording, try to use a tape deck with an external microphone to reduce the chance of picking up the internal motor of the tape recorder. Use new tapes each time you are to record, and purchase tapes that are sixty minutes or less.

Remember, you will have to listen to every second of every tape you make. Ensure you record the time, date, and location at the start of each tape.

Some of the best recordings are made with the assistance of white noise. To produce this, you can purchase a white noise generator, which can be operated close to your recording equipment, or you can adjust the volume control on your tape deck to maximum. Shop around and purchase an audio enhancement and editing computer program to help analyze your recordings.

When it comes to capturing images, any type of camera can produce results, as long as you follow some rules. The camera must be in good working order, and you should be familiar with how everything works. Keep the camera clean and free of dust. Watch for light sources (e.g. lamps, the sun, and flash), which may cause lens flare and mislead you into thinking you've captured a true anomaly. Rain, snow, moisture, and dust particles can all reflect light, especially from a camera flash. Control your camera strap and lens cover; don't let them fall in front of the lens. If you have long hair you may want to tie it back or wear a hat. Be aware that if you take photos towards shiny or reflective surfaces they will produce a glare or reflection from your flash or other light sources. When more than one investigator is photographing in an area, be sure to communicate with the others so you are not overlapping flashes into someone else's photos. If you are shooting photos outdoors, especially at night, try to include an object in the background to allow for a size and distance comparison; an open-air photo at night is almost impossible to orient yourself to. If it is cold, you have to be aware of the steam your breath will make. Never smoke anywhere near where you are shooting photographs, and in the summer watch for fireflies, which can give the illusion of slow moving, flashing orbs.

Digital cameras are great; you don't need film and they produce images immediately for your review, allowing you the advantage of finding and tracking an anomaly. However, they have one major drawback: your camera cannot produce a negative and therefore it is difficult to prove that your photo hasn't been tampered with. If you are working with a team, ensure you pair off. One should use a digital to take the majority of the photos and their teammate should use a standard SLR. This allows for two perspectives of the image, should you capture one, and also produces a negative.

When you are shooting in near or complete darkness, try to use a tripod to steady your shot, unless you are using a very high speed film and your camera apertures are designed to operate effectively in extremely low lighting levels.

Included in this guide are samples of the investigation data collection sheet, interview form, and surveillance report. These are only examples of what can be used during field investigations and are provided mainly to give you ideas for designing your own forms and reports to suit your specific needs.

DATA COLLECTION FORM

Investigator _____

Other personnel present _____

Date _____ Time commenced _____ Time completed _____

Location _____

Description _____

_____

Weather _____

Equipment used _____

Instant camera _____ 35-mm camera _____

Digital camera _____ Video camera _____

Standard surveillance _____ Wireless surveillance _____

Film type _____

Tape type _____

EMF _____ Thermometer _____ Night vision _____

Other _____

EVP _____ Micro _____ Standard _____

Reel to Reel _____

Black box _____

Microphone _____ Infraphone _____ Parabolic _____

Phenomena witnessed _____

Time _____ Duration _____

Was communication attempted? By? _____

Method _____

Results _____

Comments/Observations _____

_____

_____

Number of pages _____ Number of attachments _____

Other _____

INTERVIEW FORM

File number _____ Investigator _____

Initial contact _____ Date _____

Details of contact _____

Address _____

How many people at location _____

Name/Age/Occupation _____

Religious affiliations _____

Any pets at location _____

Any reaction _____

Age/history of location _____

When did occupants move in? _____

When did phenomena start? _____

Description of locations (add map) _____

Any recent renovations? _____

Is there any interest in the paranormal? _____

Has anyone else been notified? _____

Has the media been advised? _____

Describe events _____

Multiple witnesses _____

Normal duration of an event _____

Who seems most affected? _____

How often do these events occur? _____

How does it make you feel? _____

What do you think is going on? _____

Does everyone here agree on what is going on or is there a difference of opinion?

_____

Any tapes/photos/artifacts _____

Notes _____

_____

Photos _____ Drawings _____ Maps _____ Articles _____

Other Data _____

SURVEILLANCE REPORT

Date _____

Time _____

Investigator _____

Location _____

Area of observation _____

View/Direction _____

Equipment being used _____

Type of VCR (make/model) _____

Type/brand of tape _____

New _____

Type of camera _____

Power source _____

Diagram of wiring and hook-up of equipment _____

Day _____

Tape # _____

Observations _____

Could observable phenomena be the result of defective equipment, lights,

reflections, or interference? _____

If no, why not? _____

Tampering: explain control and security measures _____

_____

Supporting observations and witnesses _____

_____

Supporting data/Other instruments _____

_____

Comments _____

_____

_____

_____